GRAPHING CALCULATOR MANUAL

to accompany

Precalculus: Functions and Graphs
Fourth Edition
and
Precalculus: Graphical, Numerical, Algebraic
Fifth Edition

Franklin Demana
The Ohio State University
Bert K. Waits
The Ohio State University
Gregory D. Foley
Appalachian State University
Daniel Kennedy
Baylor School

Addison
Wesley

Boston San Francisco New York
London Toronto Sydney Tokyo Singapore Madrid
Mexico City Munich Paris Cape Town Hong Kong Montreal

Reproduced by Addison-Wesley Publishing Company Inc. from camera-ready copy supplied by the authors.

ISBN   0-201-70068-9

1 2 3 4 5 6 7 8 9 10 PHTH 03 02 01 00

TABLE OF CONTENTS

CHAPTER

1

Grapher Workshop

1.1   Introduction

We call this chapter a workshop to emphasize that learning the grapher requires active hands-on work. In thousands of workshop hours over the past 10 years we have helped mathematics students and instructors learn how to use hand-held graphing calculators. Our reward has been the enthusiasm and excitement of the participants as they catch on to the remarkable way that a grapher aids their learning and teaching.

As much as we would like to do it, we cannot bring the actual workshop to you. Nevertheless, with some basic knowledge and your own creativity, you can learn to use and appreciate this technology. A few hours of productive play with this powerful tool will allow you to solve mathematical problems in new ways. As you read the text, you should work through the activities and examples using your grapher. Feel free to explore its menus and features. We suggest that you refer to this workshop whenever you encounter mathematics that require you to use features of the grapher that you are unfamiliar with. The grapher is a powerful tool. With play, thought, and practice, many students have found it both useful and exciting.

1.2   Numerical Computation and Editing

First Steps

Take a moment to study the keyboard of your grapher. The keys are grouped in "zones" according to their function: scientific calculation, graphing, editing, and various menus. Locate ON. Not only is it used to turn on your grapher, but it also acts as an OFF button as its *second function*, 2nd ON.

- Practice turning your calculator on and off.

Next determine how to adjust the screen contrast, something you may need to do as lighting conditions change or battery power weakens. (You may have to check your grapher owner's manual to see how this is done.)

- Adjust your screen contrast to make the screen very dark, then very light, and finally to suit your taste.

Grapher Notes: *1. In this workshop, boxed items in small caps, such as* $\boxed{\text{TAN}}$, *suggest grapher keys. Unboxed words in small caps, such as* FUNCTION MODE, *suggest on-screen menu items. 2. Most grapher keys have multiple functions. You can access the second function of a key by first pressing the special colored* $\boxed{\text{2nd}}$ *or* $\boxed{\text{SHIFT}}$ *and its alphabetic function by pressing* $\boxed{\text{ALPHA}}$.

Performing Calculations

Computation is done on the *Home screen.*

- Try the calculations shown in Figure 1.1. Simply key in each expression, followed by $\boxed{\text{ENTER}}$ (or $\boxed{\text{EXE}}$). To find the value of log 100, use $\boxed{\text{LOG}}$. Do not enter the individual letters L, O, and G.

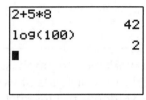

Figure 1.1

Error Messages

Don't be afraid to make a mistake! Just as pencils have erasers, graphers have delete ($\boxed{\text{DEL}}$) keys. Let's purposely make a mistake to see what happens.

- Key in 7 $\boxed{\div}$ 0, press $\boxed{\text{ENTER}}$, and observe your grapher's error message.

Error messages vary from grapher to grapher. Take a moment to read your grapher's error message. If a menu appears with a GoTo option, choose this option to "go to" the source of the error.

- Use your cursor keys ($\boxed{\blacktriangleleft}$, $\boxed{\blacktriangleright}$, $\boxed{\blacktriangle}$, and $\boxed{\blacktriangledown}$) and $\boxed{\text{DEL}}$ to change the expression from 7 ÷ 0 to 7 ÷ 2. Then enter this new expression.

Did you obtain the expected answer? If not, check your grapher owner's manual (CYGOM). (See the note below.) Take a few minutes to play with the editing features of your grapher. These few minutes could save you hours in the long run.

Grapher Note: *Keying sequences and other procedures vary somewhat from grapher to grapher, causing a need for you to "check your grapher owner's manual." We will abbreviate this instruction as* CYGOM.

Example 1   Replaying and Editing a Computation

If you deposit $500 in a savings account at a 4.5% interest rate, compounded annually, how much will you have in your account at the end of 2, 4, and 11 years?

Solution   The total value S of the investment at the end of n years is

$$S = P(1 + r)^n,$$

where r is the interest rate. Because $4.5\% = 0.045, 1 + r = 1.045$.

• Enter the expression 500×1.045^2 on the Home screen of your grapher. If your answer has unwanted decimal places, change your *display mode* to two decimal places (CYGOM if necessary) and reenter the expression, as shown in Figure 1.2.

Figure 1.2 The compound interest expression computed in
floating point mode and two decimal place *display mode*.

• *Replay* the previous entry. That is, reenter the expression without retyping the entire expression (CYGOM if necessary). Then change the exponent from 2 to 4. Repeat for the exponent 11, as shown in Figure 1.3.

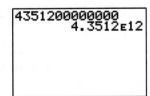

Figure 1.3 The compound interest expression computed
for three different time values.

We conclude that the values in the account are $546.01 at the end of 2 years, $596.26 after 4 years, and $811.43 after 11 years.

Scientific Notation

The U.S. national debt as of 1993 was $4,351,200,000,000.

• Enter this number of dollars on the Home screen.

Your grapher will return the value in *scientific notation* because the number is so large. (See Figure 1.4.) We interpret this result as 4.3512×10^{12} dollars or, because 10^{12} is 1 trillion, as $4.3512 trillion.

```
4351200000000
        4.3512ᴇ12
```

Figure 1.4

The ANS Feature

When doing a series of calculations, you can easily use the answer from one calculation in the next calculation.

- Carry out the calculations shown in Figure 1.5 by pressing 7 $\boxed{\times}$ 7 $\boxed{\text{ENTER}}$, then $\boxed{\times}$ 9 $\boxed{\text{ENTER}}$, and finally $\boxed{\sqrt{\ }}$ $\boxed{\text{ANS}}$ $\boxed{\text{ENTER}}$. Note in the second step of the calculation that "Ans" automatically appeared on the screen because the grapher needed a quantity to multiply by 9.

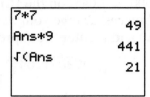

Figure 1.5

When repeating a calculation recursively, you can use the ANS feature in an extremely useful way.

- Calculate a few terms of the geometric sequence that begins with 3 and grows by a constant factor of 5 by carrying out the calculation shown in Figure 1.6.

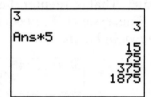

Figure 1.6

Using Variables

Another extremely helpful computational feature of the grapher is the ability to store and recall numbers as variables. The next activity illustrates using the variable x to evaluate a function at several different values of x. The activity also uses $\boxed{:}$ to string together commands. If your grapher does not have $\boxed{:}$, use $\boxed{\text{ENTER}}$ instead.

- Evaluate $f(x) = x^2 + x - 2$ at $x = 1$ by pressing

  1 $\boxed{\text{STO►}}$ $\boxed{\text{X,T,}\theta}$ $\boxed{:}$ $\boxed{\text{X,T,}\theta}$ $\boxed{x^2}$ $\boxed{+}$ $\boxed{\text{X,T,}\theta}$ $\boxed{-}$ 2 $\boxed{\text{ENTER}}$.

Then use the replaying and editing features of your grapher to evaluate $f(6)$ and $f(-8)$, as shown in Figure 1.7.

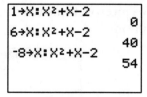

Figure 1.7

1.3 Table Building

A grapher feature even more powerful than the ability to store variables is the ability to store functions. This feature is the basis of graphing and table building. In either case the *Y= edit screen* is used to store the symbolic expressions (rules) for functions. A table can be used to evaluate a function for several different *x*-values.

- Press $\boxed{\text{Y=}}$ (or [SYMB]) to go to the Y = screen. Then press $\boxed{\text{X,T,}\theta}\boxed{x^2}\boxed{+}\boxed{\text{X,T,}\theta}\boxed{-}$ 2 $\boxed{\text{ENTER}}$. See Figure 1.8a.

- Press $\boxed{\text{TBLSET}}$ 0 $\boxed{\text{ENTER}}$ 1 $\boxed{\text{ENTER}}\boxed{\text{ENTER}}$. See Figure 1.8b. Then press $\boxed{\text{TABLE}}$. See Figure 1.8c. (This key sequence will vary from grapher to grapher. CYGOM if necessary.)

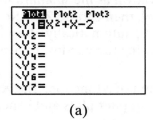
(a)
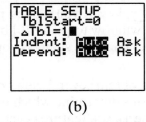
(b)
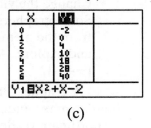
(c)

Figure 1.8 The steps in the table-building process on a grapher.

- Use the cursor keys ($\boxed{\blacktriangleright}$, $\boxed{\blacktriangleleft}$, $\boxed{\blacktriangle}$, and $\boxed{\blacktriangledown}$) to move around the table and explore. Pay attention to the readout at the bottom of the screen as you move to different "cells" in the table. What happens when you try to move the cursor off the top or bottom of the screen?

1.4 Function Graphing

Graphing and Exploring a Function

Most graphers have several graphing modes. Be sure that your grapher is in FUNCTION mode. The algebraic form for the function needs to be $f(x) = \ldots$, or $y = \ldots$.

Example 2   Graphing and Tracing along a Function

Use the FUNCTION mode to graph $f(x) = 2x + 1$. Explore the ordered pairs of the graph with the TRACE feature.

Solution   Figure 1.9 illustrates the procedure for graphing f in the window $[-6, 6]$ by $[-4, 4]$. Window is called range on some graphers.

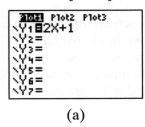
(a)
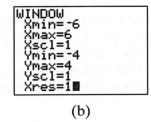
(b)
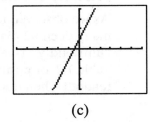
(c)

Figure 1.9 The steps in the graphing process.

- Enter $y = 2x + 1$ as shown in Figure 1.9a and the *window dimensions* as shown in Figure 1.9b. Then press $\boxed{\text{GRAPH}}$ or [PLOT] to obtain the graph shown in Figure 1.9c.

- Press ⌈TRACE⌉ to display x- and y-coordinates of points on the graph. Use ⌈▶⌉ or ⌈◀⌉ to move from point to point. See Figure 1.10. This *tracing* shows you which points of $f(x) = 2x + 1$ were plotted by the grapher.

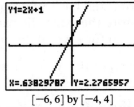

[−6, 6] by [−4, 4]

Figure 1.10 The graph of $f(x) = 2x + 1$ with the TRACE feature activated.

- Change the view dimensions to $[-10, 10]$ by $[-10, 10]$, known as the *standard window*. Some graphers have a ⌈ZOOM⌉ key. If yours does, press ⌈ZOOM⌉, then choose ZSTANDARD from the menu to set the window to $[-10, 10]$ by $[-10, 10]$ automatically. Press ⌈TRACE⌉ and explore. Are the (x, y) pairs the same as you found using the window $[-6, 6]$ by $[-4, 4]$?

A grapher allows you to obtain several views of the graph of a function. The Xmin and Xmax window dimensions determine which points the grapher plots and hence the coordinate readout when the TRACE feature is activated.

Your choice of Xmin and Xmax affects the x-coordinate readout when you trace along a graph. The reason is that the grapher screen is a rectangular array of *pixels*, short for "picture elements." The change in x-value that occurs when tracing is given by

$$\Delta x = \frac{\text{Xmax} - \text{Xmin}}{\text{Number of columns of pixels} - 1}.$$

The number of columns of pixels varies from grapher to grapher, as indicated in Table 1.1.

Table 1.1 The number of columns of pixels on various graphers

Grapher	Columns of Pixels
TI-80	63
Casio, Sharp, TI-82, TI-83	95
TI-81	96
TI-85	127
Hewlett-Packard	131
TI-92	239

Friendly Windows

As we observed in Example 2, the x-values displayed on the screen during tracing have many decimal places—for example, $x = 0.63829787$, as shown in Figure 1.10. Such "unfriendly" x-values can be avoided. You can use the [Xmin, Xmax] settings given in Table 1.2, or positive integer multiples of these settings, to guarantee a *friendly* x-coordinate readout when tracing. Windows with friendly x-coordinates are called *friendly windows.*

Table 1.2 The [Xmin, Xmax] dimensions for a basic friendly window on various graphers

Grapher	[Xmin, Xmax]
TI-80	[–3.1, 3.1]
Casio, Sharp, TI-82, TI-83	[–4.7, 4.7]
TI-81	[–4.8, 4.7]
TI-85	[–6.3, 6.3]
Hewlett-Packard	[–6.5, 6.5]
TI-92	[–11.9, 11.9]

Grapher Note: *Some graphers have a* ZDECIMAL *feature that sets* [Xmin, Xmax] *to the basic friendly settings and a* ZINTEGER *feature that can set the x-view dimensions to 10 times the basic friendly settings.*

- Graph the function $f(x) = 2x + 1$ from Example 2 in a friendly window, using the [Xmin, Xmax] settings given for your grapher in Table 1.2. Trace along the graph.

- Double the [Xmin, Xmax] and [Ymin, Ymax] settings and trace along the new view of the graph. How has the x-coordinate readout changed?

- Enter 10 times the settings given for your grapher in Table 1.2 to obtain *integer settings*. Trace to learn the reason for this name.

Square Windows

The graph of $f(x) = 2x + 1$ is a straight line with a slope of 2. You have seen several views of this graph in different windows. The apparent steepness of the graph can be quite different even though the slope is always 2.

- Graph $f(x) = 2x + 1$ in the window [–9, 9] by [–2, 2] and then in the window [–9, 9] by [–20, 20]. Compare the apparent steepness of the graph in the two windows.

In general, to obtain a graph that suggests the graph's true shape, you must choose viewing dimensions that are proportional to the dimensions of your grapher screen. Most grapher screens have a width-to-height ratio of roughly $3 : 2$. Windows whose dimensions are proportional to the physical dimensions of the grapher screen are called *square windows*. Square windows yield true shapes: They make perpendicular lines look perpendicular, squares look square, and circles look circular.

Example 3 Rounding Out a Circle

Use your grapher to plot the circle $x^2 + y^2 = 1$.

Solution First, you will need to do some algebra:

$$x^2 + y^2 = 1$$
$$y^2 = 1 - x^2$$
$$y = \pm\sqrt{1 - x^2}$$

So the graph of the circle $x^2 + y^2 = 1$ is the union of the graphs of the functions $y_1 = \sqrt{1 - x^2}$ and $y_2 = -\sqrt{1 - x^2}$.

- Graph $y_1 = \sqrt{(1 - x^2)}$ and $y_2 = -\sqrt{(1 - x^2)}$ in several windows with different x-y dimension ratios. (We used parentheses around $1 - x^2$ because you will need them to enter the functions onto the Y= edit screen.) Continue until you obtain a graph that appears circular. *Note:* Gaps may appear near the x-axis.

- Graph $y_1 = \sqrt{1 - x^2}$ and $y_2 = -\sqrt{1 - x^2}$ in a square, friendly window.

Grapher Note: *Some graphers have a* ZSQUARE *feature that adjusts the window dimensions to make them match the physical proportions of the screen.*

Figure 1.11 shows three views. Only the view in part (a) looks circular because only in part (a) are the window dimensions proportional to the physical dimensions of the screen.

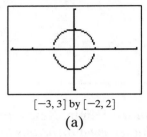
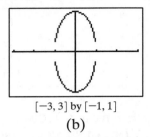
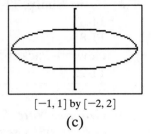

[−3, 3] by [−2, 2]	[−3, 3] by [−1, 1]	[−1, 1] by [−2, 2]
(a)	(b)	(c)

Figure 1.11 The graph of a circle in (a) a square window and (b and c) nonsquare windows.

Square, friendly, or standard windows are not always ideal. Example 4 illustrates that window dimensions may need to be exaggerated to reveal the important features of a graph.

Example 4 Finding Key Features of a Graph

Graph $f(x) = x^2(x + 7)^3$, using Xmin $= -10$ and Xmax $= 10$. Try various [Ymin, Ymax] settings.

Solution Figure 1.12 shows three possible views.

• Try the windows shown in Figure 1.12 and several others of your own choosing. Continue until you convince yourself that you have observed all the important features of $f(x) = x^2(x + 7)^3$ on the interval [−10, 10].

Note that the view in part (c) shows more features of the graph than either part (a) or part (b) and hence is the best view of the three. Further investigation of the graph in other windows should reveal no other major features on the interval [−10, 10].

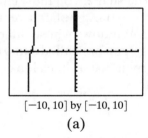
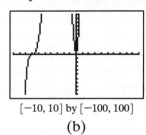
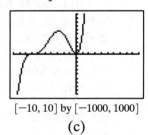

[−10, 10] by [−10, 10]	[−10, 10] by [−100, 100]	[−10, 10] by [−1000, 1000]
(a)	(b)	(c)

Figure 1.12 The graph of the same function in three different viewing windows.

Example 5 is designed to familiarize you with 12 basic graphs that are used in the textbook and are important as models in many fields of endeavor. You should learn these graphs by heart! That is, you should be able to sketch any of them quickly at any time without a great deal of thought, without doing any hand computation, and without using your grapher.

Example 5 Touring a Gallery of Basic Functions

Plot and explore the 12 graphs shown in Figure 1.13.

Solution You may need to do some searching on your grapher keyboard or dig through some menus to find all these functions (CYGOM). You should use function notation—for example, abs (X) rather than abs X—even though your grapher may be forgiving.

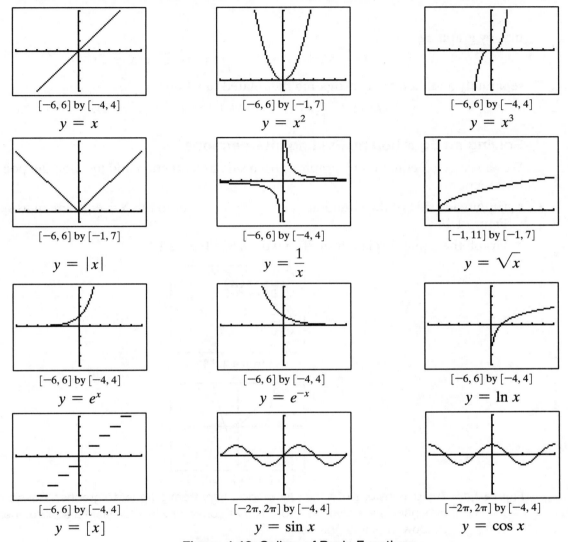

Figure 1.13 Gallery of Basic Functions

- Graph all but the sine and cosine functions with the windows indicated in Figure 1.13. Regraph each function for other window dimensions, including standard, friendly, and square. Explore with TRACE.

- Graph the greatest integer function in CONNECTED mode and then in DOT mode. Which produces the better graph? Why?

- Graph the sine and cosine functions in DEGREE mode and then in RADIAN mode. Note that the graphs in Figure 1.13 are based on the use of RADIAN mode.

Grapher Note: *Some graphers have* ZTRIG *that automatically sets desirable window dimensions for viewing trigonometric functions.*

You should practice making hand-drawn sketches of the 12 basic functions until you can do them from memory.

1.5   Graphical Problem Solving

In this section we explore various grapher methods for solving equations and analyzing the graphical behavior of functions, so you should set your grapher to FUNCTION mode. We begin by showing how to solve equations graphically, using the example

$$|x| = x^2 + x - 2,$$

first by graphing

$$f(x) = |x| \quad \text{and} \quad g(x) = x^2 + x - 2$$

separately and then by investigating the related function

$$h(x) = f(x) - g(x) = |x| - (x^2 + x - 2).$$

Solving an Equation by Finding Intersections

We can solve an equation by graphing each side as a function and locating the points of intersection.

- Enter each side of the equation $|x| = x^2 + x - 2$ onto the Y= edit screen as shown in Figure 1.14.

- Graph the equations in a friendly window. See Figure 1.15.

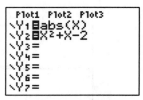

Figure 1.14

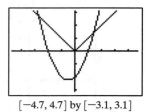

$[-4.7, 4.7]$ by $[-3.1, 3.1]$

Figure 1.15 The dimensions of a friendly window vary from grapher to grapher. Possible *x* dimensions are given in Table 1.2. ZDECIMAL or ZINTEGER yield a square, friendly window on some graphers.

The graph of *f* is V-shaped and the graph of *g* is an upward opening parabola. They have two points of intersection. Thus the equation $|x| = x^2 + x - 2$ has two solutions. These solutions are the *x*-coordinates (one positive and one negative) of the two points of intersection.

- Trace along either graph to approximate the positive solution, that is, to estimate the *x*-coordinate of the point of intersection in the first quadrant.

To get a better approximation for the positive solution we can *zoom in* by picking smaller and smaller windows that contain the point of intersection in the first quadrant. Three common ways to zoom in are to

1. change the WINDOW settings manually;

2. use ZOOMBOX, which lets you use the cursor to select the opposite corners of a "box" to define a new window; and

3. use ZOOMIN, which magnifies the graph around the cursor location by a factor that you can set.

- Practice each of the three types of zooming (CYGOM if necessary). Trace after each zoom step, as shown in Figure 1.16.

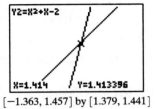

$[-1.363, 1.457]$ by $[1.379, 1.441]$

Figure 1.16 One possible view of the graphs after some zooming, with the TRACE feature activated.

Most graphers have an INTERSECTION feature that can be used to automate the process of solving equations graphically without adjusting the viewing window dimensions.

- Graph the equations of Figure 1.14 in a friendly window (Figure 1.15). Then use the INTERSECTION feature to locate the point of intersection in the first quadrant, as shown in Figure 1.17.

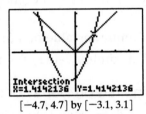

$[-4.7, 4.7]$ by $[-3.1, 3.1]$

Figure 1.17

Solving the equation $|x| = x^2 + x - 2$ algebraically reveals that the positive solution is $x = \sqrt{2} = 1.4142\ldots$, which confirms the graphical solution.

Solving by Finding x-Intercepts

To solve an equation of the form $f(x) = g(x)$, we can solve $f(x) - g(x) = 0$. Then the problem becomes one of finding where the functions $y = f - g$ and $y = 0$ intersect, or simply the x-intercepts of $y = f - g$. For example, to solve the equation $|x| = x^2 + x - 2$, we can find the x-intercepts of

$$y = h(x) = f(x) - g(x) = |x| - (x^2 + x - 2).$$

- Load the Y= edit screen, as shown in Figure 1.18a, selecting only $y_3 = y_1 - y_2 = \text{abs}\,(x) - (x^2 + x - 2)$ to be graphed.
- Graph y_3 in a friendly window, as shown in Figure 1.18b.
- The x-intercepts are also the "zeros" of the equation. Use the ZERO feature (CYGOM if necessary) to locate the negative x-intercept, as shown in Figure 1.18c.

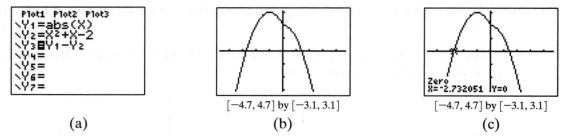

(a)   [−4.7, 4.7] by [−3.1, 3.1]   [−4.7, 4.7] by [−3.1, 3.1]
                              (b)   (c)

Figure 1.18 Finding a solution of an equation by finding an *x*-intercept of the difference function.

Studying Graph Behavior

As you have seen, TRACE allows you to move from pixel to pixel on a graph with the coordinates of the points displayed to illustrate the numerical behavior of the function. For example, you can see whether the *y*-coordinate increases, decreases, or remains constant as *x* increases. ZOOMIN permits a "close-up" examination of the *local behavior* of graphs.

Three other grapher features are useful for investigating graph behavior (CYGOM if necessary).

1. VALUE evaluates a function for a given domain value, which often avoids the need for a friendly window.

2. MINIMUM finds a local minimum value of a function and the associated domain value.

3. MAXIMUM finds a local maximum value of a function and the associated domain value.

Example 6 Investigating Graph Behavior

Graph $f(x) = x^3 + 2x^2 - 5x - 6$ and study its behavior.

Solution Do the following on your grapher.

• Graph $y = f(x)$ in the standard window. Trace over until $x \approx -3.4$, as shown in Figure 1.19a. Then trace from left to right. Observe whether the function values (*y*-coordinates) increase, decrease, or remain constant as *x* increases.

• The graph appears to show that $f(2) = 0$, but TRACE fails to give a *y* value for $x = 2$. Use VALUE to find $f(2)$, as shown in Figure 1.19b.

• To determine precisely the intervals on which *f* is increasing or decreasing, locate the domain values at which the local maximums and minimums occur. Use MAXIMUM and MINIMUM to find these values. Figure 1.19c shows the result of using the MAXIMUM feature.

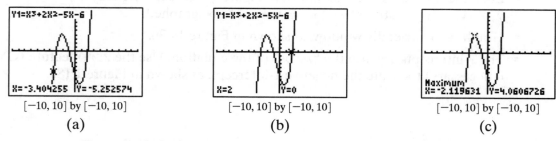

[−10, 10] by [−10, 10]   [−10, 10] by [−10, 10]   [−10, 10] by [−10, 10]
        (a)   (b)   (c)

Figure 1.19 Exploring a graph with (a) TRACE, (b) VALUE, and (c) MAXIMUM.

- Zoom in around the points that correspond to the local maximum and the local minimum. Describe the graph's behavior near each of these points.

What other behaviors of graphs can you study with the features of your grapher?

1.6   Parametric and Polar Graphing

Parametric Graphing

To graph parametric equations, set your grapher to PARAMETRIC mode. In PARAMETRIC mode, pressing $\boxed{\text{X,T,}\theta}$ will yield the independent variable t. The parametric equations

$$x(t) = \ldots, \qquad y(t) = \ldots$$

are entered in the form $x_1(t) = \ldots, y_1(t) = \ldots$ on the Y= edit screen.

Example 7   Graphing Parametric Equations

Graph the parametric equations.

$$x = t^2, \qquad y = t - 1 \qquad \text{for } -2 \le t \le 2$$

Solution   Follow these steps:

- Enter the parametric equations on the Y= edit screen, as shown in Figure 1.20.

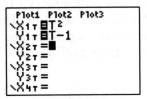

```
Plot1  Plot2  Plot3
\X₁ᴛ█T²
 Y₁ᴛ█T-1
\X₂ᴛ=█
 Y₂ᴛ=
\X₃ᴛ=
 Y₃ᴛ=
\X₄ᴛ=
```

Figure 1.20

- Set the WINDOW dimensions shown in Figure 1.21. You will need to scroll down to see the entire menu given in Figure 1.21 because it has too many lines..

```
WINDOW
 Tmin=-2
 Tmax=2
 Tstep=.1
 Xmin=-4.7
 Xmax=4.7
 Xscl=1
↓Ymin=-3.1█
```

Figure 1.21 Facsimile of the WINDOW screen set for plotting the parametric equations.

Tstep on the parametric WINDOW menu sets the step size between the successive t-values that the grapher uses to compute and plot (x, y) pairs. In this case, the Tstep of 0.1 will yield 40 steps from the Tmin of -2 to the Tmax of 2. Thus 41 points will be calculated and plotted, with the points corresponding to

$$t = -2.0, -1.9, -1.8, -1.7, \ldots, 1.9, 2.0.$$

- Press $\boxed{\text{GRAPH}}$ or $\lceil\text{PLOT}\rceil$ to obtain the graph shown in Figure 1.22.

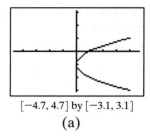

$[-4.7, 4.7]$ by $[-3.1, 3.1]$

(a)

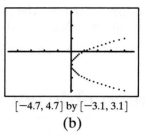

$[-4.7, 4.7]$ by $[-3.1, 3.1]$

(b)

Figure 1.22 The graph in (a) CONNECTED mode and (b) DOT mode.

- Use TRACE to explore the graph numerically. Note that the values of the parameter t and the coordinates x and y are all shown on the screens in Figure 1.23.

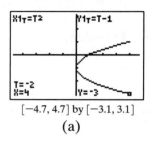

$[-4.7, 4.7]$ by $[-3.1, 3.1]$

(a)

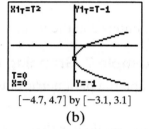

$[-4.7, 4.7]$ by $[-3.1, 3.1]$

(b)

Figure 1.23 Two views of the parametric curve with TRACE activated.

Figures 1.22 and 1.23 show only a piece of the parabola $x = (y + 1)^2$ rather than the complete parabola for this viewing window. The parametric WINDOW menu allows you to choose a part of the graph by setting Tmin and Tmax. Do you see why? If not, experiment with the Tmin and Tmax settings until you do.

Polar Graphing

To graph polar equations set your grapher to POLAR mode. Pressing $\boxed{\text{x,t,}\theta}$ will yield the independent variable θ.

Example 8 Graphing Polar Equations

Simultaneously graph $r = 9 \sin 5\theta$ *and* $r = 9$.

Solution Follow these steps:

- Set your grapher to SIMULTANEOUS and RADIAN modes. Then enter the polar equations on the Y= edit screen, as shown in Figure 1.24.

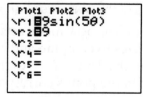

Figure 1.24

- Set the WINDOW dimensions to

$$\theta\text{min} = 0, \qquad \theta\text{max} = 2\pi, \qquad \theta\text{step} = \pi/24,$$

using the standard dimension of $[-10, 10]$ by $[-10, 10]$ for x and y. (On some graphers, you can obtain these settings by using ZSTANDARD.)

- Press GRAPH or ⌈PLOT⌉ to obtain the graphs shown in Figure 1.25.

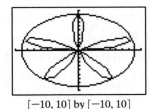

[−10, 10] by [−10, 10]

Figure 1.25 The circle $r = 9$ and the 5-petaled rose $r = 9 \sin 5\theta$.

- Trace along the two polar curves.
- Set θ max $= \pi$. Then use ZSQUARE to square the viewing window. If no such command is available on your grapher, reset the x-dimensions of the WINDOW menu by hand. Figure 1.26 shows the result.

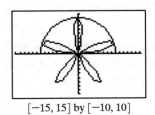

[−15, 15] by [−10, 10]

Figure 1.26

Note that the entire rose curve is plotted for the interval $0 \le \theta \le \pi$. Explore the effect of changing the 5 in the equation $r = 9 \sin 5\theta$ to another number.

1.7   Curve Fitting and Statistics

A grapher can help you organize, process, and analyze data, as well as compute and plot models for paired data. The procedures for data analysis and curve fitting vary a great deal from grapher to grapher (CYGOM for details).

Example 9 Plotting and Fitting Data

Plot the national debt data given in Table 1.3, find a model for the data, and then overlay a graph of the model on the scatter plot.

Table 1.3 U.S. Public Debt, 1950–1990

Year	Debt (Billions of dollars)
1950	256.1
1960	284.1
1970	370.1
1975	533.2
1980	907.7
1985	1,823.1
1990	3,233.3

Source: The World Almanac and Book of Facts (1995, Mahwah, N.J.: Funk & Wagnalls), p. 109.

Solution Follow these steps:

- Enter the data shown in Table 1.3 into the statistical memory of your grapher, as shown in Figure 1.27a.

- Set an appropriate window for the data, letting *x* be the year and *y* be the amount of the debt, as shown in Figure 1.27b.

- Make a scatter plot of the data, as shown in Figure 1.27c.

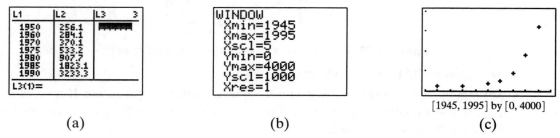

(a)   (b)   (c)

Figure 1.27 The steps involved in making a scatter plot on a grapher.

Most graphers have several regression options. Typically, linear, quadratic, exponential, logarithmic, and power functions are available as regression models. Some graphers offer other options. The following activity illustrates quadratic regression. That is, we find a quadratic function that closely fits the given data.

- Choose the QUADRATIC option from your grapher's regression menu. Use the first column of data for the *x*-values and the second column as *y*-values. The grapher should return approximate coefficients for the quadratic regression equation, as shown in Figure 1.28a.

- Load the regression equation onto the Y= edit screen, as shown in Fiugre 1.28b.

- Press GRAPH or PLOT to obtain the graph in Figure 1.28c, which shows both the scatter plot and the graph of the regression equation.

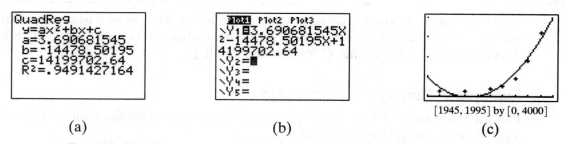

(a)   (b)   (c)

Figure 1.28 The steps involved in fitting a quadratic function to a scatter plot.

Repeat the steps to find and graph other regression equations for the data.

Most graphers offer a variety of statistical plots, often including histograms, boxplots, and line graphs. In addition, graphers can carry out many types of statistical computations (CYGOM for details).

1.8 Matrix Calculations

A grapher can perform many matrix operations, thus avoiding the tedium of hand computation. Matrix procedures vary somewhat from grapher to grapher (CYGOM for details).

- Place matrix A on the Home screen (Figure 1.29a) and compute its determinant (Figure 1.29b).

(a) (b)

Figure 1.29 (a) Matrix entry and (b) matrix display and determinant calculation.

- Compute the inverse of matrix A. You may need to scroll, using $\boxed{\blacktriangleright}$ in order to see the entire answer (Figure 1.30).

(a) (b)

Figure 1.30 (a) Computing the inverse of matrix A and (b) scrolling.

Grapher Note: *In Figure 1.30a, we used the* FRAC *feature to convert the decimal entries of* A^{-1} *to fractions.*

- Enter the matrix $B = \begin{pmatrix} 12 \\ 9 \\ -13 \end{pmatrix}$ into the matrix editor of your grapher (Figure 1.31a).

- Compute the product $A^{-1} \cdot B$ on the Home screen (Figure 1.31b).

(a) (b)

Figure 1.31 (a) Entering a column matrix and (b) multiplying matrices.

Graphers have other matrix features. Most importantly, many graphers can perform elementary row operations on a matrix.

1.9 Grapher Insights and Caveats

Limitations of Grapher Computations

Grapher computations are limited in *magnitude* and *relative accuracy*. Numbers less than the lower magnitude limit are rounded to zero. Numbers greater than or equal to the upper magnitude limit yield *overflow errors*.

Regarding relative error, some graphers store only the first 13 significant digits of a number (the rest of the number is rounded off) and they display at most 10 digits. To see this in action,

- Enter $(2/3 - 1/3) - 1/3$ on your grapher.

We know that $(2/3 - 1/3) - 1/3 = 0$, but older graphers will not give 0 as the final result. What steps in the grapher computation could have produced this result? Explain.

How a Grapher Draws a Function Graph

All graphers produce graphs, or plots, by lighting pixels on a liquid crystal display (LCD). Figure 1.33a shows the graph of a line on an LCD, and Figure 1.33b shows how it might appear under a magnifying glass. When the grapher is in CONNECTED mode, the plotted pixels are connected by "line segments" of pixels. When in DOT mode, the pixels are left unconnected.

(a)   (b)

Figure 1.33 (a) The graph of a line on an LCD and (b) how it looks under magnification.

Limitations of Grapher Plotting

Grapher plotting is limited by roundoff error in the calculation of the y-coordinates from the function formula. More significantly, grapher plotting is limited because, for each point plotted, a pixel is rarely centered on the LCD at the exact vertical location corresponding to the y-coordinate of the point.

Despite these limitations, graphers can quickly produce accurate graphs for most functions described in this book if the viewing dimensions are chosen appropriately. It takes mathematical and grapher experience to get good at choosing windows. You will develop this skill over time as you go through the workshop exercises and the rest of the book.

Interpreting Grapher Plots

As Examples 3 and 4 illustrated, a grapher plot may be misleading or incomplete. (See Figures 1.11 and 1.12.) True visualization occurs in the "mind's eye" when you use the information gained from a grapher together with your mathematical knowledge to obtain a mental image of the mathematical graph. To communicate this mental visualization to another person, however, you must learn to describe and draw graphs accurately. When recording a graph on paper, you should normally add suggestive arrowheads and label axes, key points, and other pertinent information. Figure 1.34 shows how two rather misleading views of a complicated graph can be combined into a single recorded graph. This is a skill to strive for as you work with the grapher.

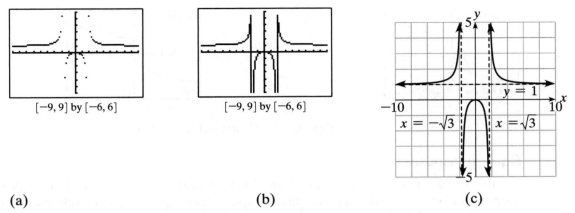

$[-9, 9]$ by $[-6, 6]$ $[-9, 9]$ by $[-6, 6]$

(a)   (b)   (c)

Figure 1.34 The graph of $y = x^2/(x^2 - 3)$ as shown (a and b) on a grapher and (c) on paper.

1.10   Viewing Window Summary

Choosing a Viewing Window

You need experience and mathematical expectations to choose appropriate viewing windows. One approach is to start with the *standard window* of $[-10, 10]$ by $[-10, 10]$ and adjust the y-dimensions.

Some windows may show more features of a graph than others. The view on the right shows the key features of the graph; the other two views do not.

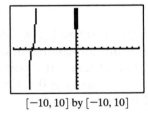 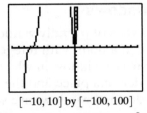 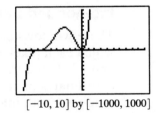

$[-10, 10]$ by $[-10, 10]$ $[-10, 10]$ by $[-100, 100]$ $[-10, 10]$ by $[-1000, 1000]$

Figure 1.35 Three views of $f(x) = x^2(x + 7)^3$.

Friendly Windows

Your choice of Xmin and Xmax affect the x-coordinate readout when you *trace* along a graph. You can use the [Xmin, Xmax] settings given in the table, or positive integer multiples of these settings, to guarantee a *friendly* x-coordinate readout when tracing. Windows with friendly x-coordinates are called *friendly windows*.

Table 1.4 The [Xmin, Xmax] dimensions for a basic friendly window on various graphers.

Grapher	[Xmin, Xmax]
TI-80	[–3.1, 3.1]
Casio, Sharp, TI-82, TI-83	[–4.7, 4.7]
TI-81	[–4.8, 4.7]
TI-85	[–6.3, 6.3]
Hewlett-Packard	[–6.5, 6.5]
TI-92	[–11.9, 11.9]

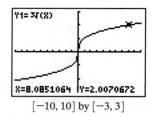

[−10, 10] by [−3, 3]

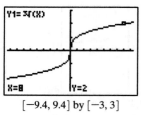

[−9.4, 9.4] by [−3, 3]

Figure 1.36 Graphs of $f(x) = \sqrt[3]{x}$

Square Windows

A *square window* is a window that shows the true shape of a graph. Such a window makes perpendicular lines look perpendicular, a square look square, and a circle look circular. A square window has the same proportions as your grapher screen. Many grapher screens have a width-to-height ratio of 3 : 2. Most graphers have a built-in feature for squaring windows.

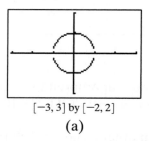

[−3, 3] by [−2, 2]

(a)

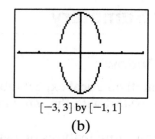

[−3, 3] by [−1, 1]

(b)

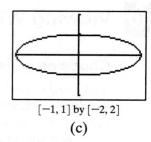

[−1, 1] by [−2, 2]

(c)

Figure 1.37 Three views of the circle $x^2 + y^2 = 1$.

Integer and Decimal Windows

These windows are special types of friendly windows. An *integer window* is a window in which each pixel is centered at a point with integer coordintes and the change in both x and y is 1. A *decimal window* is a window in which each pixel is centered at a point with coordinates of at most one decimal place and the change in both x and y is 0.1. On most graphers, both integer and decimal windows are square and friendly.

1.11 Exercises for Chapter 1

The exercises are correlated with the sections of the Grapher Workshop. If any give you difficulty, resolve it by consulting either your owner's manual or your instructor.

Numerical Computation and Editing

In Exercises 1–6, use a grapher to evaluate the expression.

1. 600×1.075^2
2. 1.3^5
3. $\log (1/10)$
4. $|-7|$
5. $\sqrt[3]{64}$
6. $\sqrt[4]{81}$

In Exercises 7 and 8, use ANS.

7. Calculate the first seven terms in the geometric sequence that begins with 2 and grows by a constant factor of 6: 2, 12, 72, ...

8. Calculate the first seven terms in the arithmetic sequence that begins with 4 and grows by a constant 9: 4, 13, 22, ...

In Exercises 9 and 10, use replay.

9. Evaluate $f(x) = x^2 + x - 2$ at $x = -3, -2.5, 3$.

10. Evaluate $g(t) = 2t^3 - |5t|$ at $t = -2, 3.4, 7$.

Table Building

In Exercises 11–14, make a table with the following inputs.

  a. $x = -3, -2, -1, \ldots, 3$

  b. $x = 0, 1, 2, \ldots, 6$

  c. $x = -10, -5, 0, \ldots, 20$

11. $f(x) = x^2 + 15$

12. $f(x) = \ln (x^2 + 1)$

13. $f(x) = |x - 2|$

14. $f(x) = \sqrt[3]{x^2 + x - 2}$

Function Graphing

In Exercises 15–20, graph the function in each type of window.

  a. The standard window

  b. A square window containing the standard window

  c. A friendly window using TRACE to support the friendly x-coordinate readout

  d. A window that is both square and friendly

15. $y = 3x - 2$

16. $y = -\frac{1}{2}x + 3$

17. $y = 1 - x^2$

18. $y = 2x^2 - 3x + 1$

19. $y = |x + 2|$

20. $y = \sqrt{9 - x^2}$

In Exercises 21 and 22, explain any differences in the two modes.

21. Enter and graph

  $y_1 = 2x + 1$;

  $y_2 = 2x + 2$;

  $y_3 = 2x + 3$.

  Switch between SEQUENTIAL and SIMULTANEOUS modes and draw the graphs again.

22. Graph $y = 3x - 1$. Switch between CONNECTED and DOT modes and draw the graph again.

In Exercises 23 and 24, find a window that reveals the key features of the function. How many x-intercepts does the graph have?

23. $y = x^2(x - 12)$

24. $y = x(x + 3)^2(x + 14)$

Graphical Problem Solving

In Exercises 25–28, solve the equation by

    a. finding intersections.

    b. finding x-intercepts.

25. $|x| = \frac{1}{2}x + 1$

26. $|x - 3| = -\frac{1}{2}x + 4$

27. $x - 2 = 1 - x^2$

28. $x - 3 = x^2 - 5$

In Exercises 29 and 30, (a) find a viewing window that reveals the key features of the graph, and (b) find the local maximum and minimum values.

29. $y = x^2(x - 12)$

30. $y = x(x + 3)^2(x + 14)$

Parametric and Polar Graphing

In Exercises 31–34, use PARAMETRIC mode.

31. Enter

$$x(t) = t, \qquad y(t) = t.$$

Predict what will happen as a result of the WINDOW settings for t. Then graph and compare with your prediction.

    a. Tmin $= -10$, Tmax $= 10$, Tstep $= 0.1$

    b. Tmin $= 0$, Tmax $= 10$, Tstep $= 0.1$

    c. Tmin $= -10$, Tmax $= 0$, Tstep $= 0.1$

    d. Tmin $= -10$, Tmax $= 10$, Tstep $= 1$

    e. Tmin $= -5$, Tmax $= 5$, Tstep $= 1$

    f. Tmin $= 10$, Tmax $= -10$, Tstep $= -0.1$

32. Graph

$$x_1(t) = t, \qquad y_1(t) = 2t;$$
$$x_2(t) = 2t, \qquad y_2(t) = t,$$

with Tmin $= -10$, Tmax $= 10$, Tstep $= 0.1$. Predict what the graphs will look like. Then graph and compare with your prediction.

33. Graph

$$x_1(t) = 2t, \qquad y_1(t) = t^2,$$

with Tmin $= -10$, Tmax $= 10$, Tstep $= 0.1$.

34. Graph
$$x_1(t) = 2t, \qquad y_1(t) = t^2;$$
$$x_2(t) = y_1(t), \quad y_2(t) = x_1(t),$$
with Tmin $= -10$, Tmax $= 10$, Tstep $= 0.1$.

In Exercises 35–38, use POLAR and RADIAN modes.

35. Graph $r = 6$ in a square window. Switch between CONNECTED and DOT modes and graph again.

36. Graph $r = 2 \cos \theta$ in a square window. Switch between CONNECTED and DOT modes and graph again.

37. Graph $r_1 = 2$ and $r_2 = 5$. Switch between SEQUENTIAL and SIMULTANEOUS modes and graph again.

38. Graph $r_1 = 2$ and $r_2 = 2 \cos 3\theta$. Switch beween SEQUENTIAL and SIMULTANEOUS modes and graph again.

Curve Fitting and Statistics

In Exercises 39 and 40, use the data in Table 1.5.

Table 1.5 Official Census Population (in millions of persons), 1900–1990

Year	Florida	Pennsylvania
1900	0.5	6.3
1910	0.8	7.7
1920	1.0	8.7
1930	1.5	9.6
1940	1.9	9.9
1950	2.7	10.5
1960	5.0	11.3
1970	6.8	11.8
1980	9.7	11.9
1990	12.9	11.9

Source: U.S. Census Bureau as reported in *The World Almanac and Book of Facts* (1995, Mahwah, N.J.: Funk & Wagnalls), p. 377.

39. a. Enter the Florida population data into the statistical memory of your grapher.

   b. Set an appropriate window for the data and make a scatter plot.

   c. Choose the EXPONENTIAL option from your grapher's regression menu to find the constants in the regression equation.

   d. Load the regression equation onto the Y $=$ edit screen and overlay the graph of the regression equation on the scatter plot.

40. a. Enter the Pennsylvania population data into the statistical memory of your grapher.

   b. Set an appropriate window for the data and make a scatter plot.

   c. Choose the LINEAR option from your grapher's regression menu to find the coefficients for the linear regression equation.

d. Load the regression equation onto the $Y =$ edit screen and overlay the graph of the regression equation on the scatter plot.

Matrix Calculations

In Exercises 41 and 42, perform the computations.

41. a. Enter the matrix

$$A = \begin{pmatrix} 1 & -3 \\ 5 & 2 \end{pmatrix}$$

   into the matrix editor of your grapher and compute its determinant.

   b. Compute the inverse of matrix A.

   c. Enter the matrix

$$B = \begin{pmatrix} -1 \\ 12 \end{pmatrix}$$

   into the matrix editor of your grapher and compute the product $A^{-1} \cdot B$.

42. a. Enter the matrix

$$A = \begin{pmatrix} 4 & 2 & -1 \\ 1 & -1 & 0 \\ 0 & 3 & 5 \end{pmatrix}$$

   into the matrix editor of your grapher and compute its determinant.

   b. Compute the inverse of matrix A.

   c. Enter the matrix

$$B = \begin{pmatrix} 15 \\ 2 \\ -2 \end{pmatrix}$$

   into the matrix editor of your grapher and compute the product $A^{-1} \cdot B$.

Grapher Insights and Caveats

In Exercises 43 and 44, sketch the graph.

43. Graph

$$y = \frac{(x + 3)^2}{x(x + 4)}$$

   in CONNECTED and DOT modes and then sketch the graph on paper.

44. Graph

$$y = \frac{x(x - 3)}{(x - 1)(x + 4)}$$

   in CONNECTED and DOT modes and then sketch the graph on paper.

2

TI-82, TI-83, and TI-83 Plus Graphing Calculators

These three graphing calculators are versatile tools for exploring mathematics. In addition to all of the features of a scientific calculator, they have large-screen computation and programming capabilities and built-in software for working with graphs, tables, lists, matrices, sequences, probability, and statistics. Hence, these calculators are actually powerful, user-friendly hand-held computers.

This chapter is designed to familiarize you with many aspects of these calculators. The three models are so similar that in most cases you can follow the same instructions, and we will refer to "your calculator," rather than the particular model number. When they do differ, specific instructions will be given for the TI-82, TI-83, and the TI-83 Plus. Also, unless otherwise noted, both the TI-83 and TI-83 Plus will be referred to as the TI-83.

Have the calculator out and "on" so that you can work through the examples as you read this chapter. Feel free to explore the menus and features of your calculator. A few hours of productive play can help you reach a comfort level so that you can readily solve problems using this powerful tool.

2.1 Getting Started

2.1.1 Exploring the Keyboard

Take a minute to study the keys on your calculator. There are 10 rows of keys, each with five keys, except for the four specially arranged cursor-movement keys. These keys are divided into three zones.

- **Row 1**
  Used for graphing and table building.

- **Rows 2, 3, and 4**
  Used for accessing menus and editing.

- **Rows 5–10**
  Used like those on a scientific calculator.

Thinking in terms of these three zones will help you find keys on your calculator.

2.1.2 Using the Multipurpose ON Key

The On key ON is in the lower left-hand corner of the keyboard. It is used to do the following:

- Turn on the calculator.

- Interrupt graphing if you want to stop before a graph is completely drawn.

- Interrupt program execution to "break out" of a program.

- Turn off the calculator. To do this, press

$$\boxed{\text{2nd}} \quad \boxed{\text{ON}}.$$

Note that the word OFF is written in colored letters just above $\boxed{\text{ON}}$ and that the color of the letters matches that of $\boxed{\text{2nd}}$. In the future, we say, "press $\boxed{\text{2nd}} \,\boxed{\text{OFF}}$."

To prolong the life of the batteries, your calculator automatically turns itself off after several minutes have elapsed without any activity. To turn on your calculator in these circumstances, press

$$\boxed{\text{ON}}.$$

Your calculator will turn on and return you to the screen on which you were working when it turned itself off.

2.1.3 Adjusting the Screen Contrast

You can adjust the screen contrast as needed, choosing from 10 contrast settings that range from 0 (the lightest) to 9 (the darkest).

To darken the screen,
  1. press and release $\boxed{\text{2nd}}$ and then
  2. press and hold $\boxed{\blacktriangle}$.

To lighten the screen,
  1. press and release $\boxed{\text{2nd}}$ and then
  2. press and hold $\boxed{\blacktriangledown}$.

If you find it necessary to set the contrast at 8 or 9, it is probably time to change your batteries. (Your calculator uses four AAA batteries.) If after you change the batteries the screen is too dark, simply adjust contrast following the steps outlined above.

2.2   Calculating and Editing

2.2.1 Returning to the Home Screen

Computation is done on the Home screen. To help you remember how to get to the Home screen from other screens and menus, remember the sentence, "Quit to go Home." This means that if you get lost in a menu and want to return to the Home screen, press

$$\boxed{\text{2nd}} \,\boxed{\text{QUIT}}.$$

($\boxed{\text{QUIT}}$ is the second function of $\boxed{\text{MODE}}$ located to the right of $\boxed{\text{2nd}}$.) If your calculator does not respond to this command, it is probably busy graphing or running a program. In this case, press

$$\boxed{\text{ON}} \text{ and then } \boxed{\text{2nd}} \,\boxed{\text{QUIT}}.$$

2.2.2 Performing Simple Calculations

1. To compute $2 + 5 \times 8$, press:

$$2 \,\boxed{+}\, 5 \,\boxed{\times}\, 8 \,\boxed{\text{ENTER}}.$$

Your screen should look like Figure 2.1.

2. Find the value of log(100) by pressing
   - on the TI-82 $\boxed{\text{LOG}} \,\boxed{(}\, 100 \,\boxed{)}\, \boxed{\text{ENTER}}$, or
   - on the TI-83 $\boxed{\text{LOG}}\, 100 \,\boxed{)}\, \boxed{\text{ENTER}}$.

Note that on the TI-83 the left parenthesis automatically appears after pressing $\boxed{\text{LOG}}$. Your screen should look like Figure 2.2.

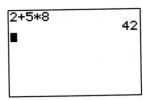

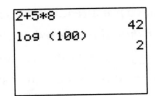

Figure 2.1   **Figure 2.2**

Note: Do not type the letters L, O, and G. The calculator would interpret this as implied multiplication of the variables L, O, and G.

2.2.3 Working with Error Messages

Your calculator knows the difference between the binary operation of subtraction (the blue $\boxed{-}$) and the additive inverse, or "sign change," operation (the gray or white $\boxed{(-)}$). To learn how the calculator handles errors related to these keys, let's purposely make a mistake. Enter the following key sequence:

$$7 \boxed{+} \boxed{-} 4 \boxed{\text{ENTER}}.$$

Your calculator should respond as shown in Figure 2.3. In this case the *error message* indicates you have made a syntax error and have two choices. This ERROR MESSAGE menu is typical of all numbered menus on your calculator. To select an item from a numbered menu, do either of the following:

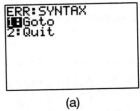

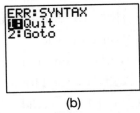

(a)   (b)

Figure 2.3 The ERROR MESSAGE menu on the (a) TI-82 and (b) TI-83.

a. press the number to the left of the choice you want—this is the fastest way—or

b. position the cursor next to your choice and press $\boxed{\text{ENTER}}$.

To return to the Home screen (Remember, "Quit to go Home."), press

$$\boxed{\text{2nd}} \boxed{\text{QUIT}},$$

or press the number that corresponds to $\boxed{\text{QUIT}}$ on your calculator. Choose Quit.

The screen should look like Figure 2.4, with a flashing cursor below the 7.

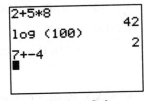

Figure 2.4

To return to the ERROR MESSAGE menu (see Fig. 2.3), press

$$\boxed{\text{ENTER}}.$$

Selecting the Goto option at this point causes the cursor to "go to" the source of the error and clears the Home screen of all data except the expression that contains the error. Generally, the Goto option will help you find your error.

1. If you have not already done so, choose the Goto option now.

The cursor should flash on the subtraction symbol.

2. Press [(−)] to overwrite the subtraction symbol with a negative sign.

3. Press [ENTER] to re-execute the calculation.

You should obtain the expected result: 3.

2.2.4 Editing Expressions

Using Last Entry. When you press [ENTER] on the Home screen to evaluate an expression or execute an instruction, the expression or instruction is stored with other previous entries in a storage area called the Last Entry Stack. You can recall a prior entry from the Last Entry Stack, edit it, and then execute the edited instruction, as the following example illustrates.

Example 1 Doubling an Investment's Value

Problem You deposit $500 in a savings account with a 4.75% annual percentage rate (APR), compounded monthly. How long will it take for your investment to double in value?

Solution Because 4.75≠5 and 100÷5=20, you might make an initial guess of 20 years. To check the guess, do the following:

1. Press [2nd] [QUIT] to return to the Home screen, if necessary.

2. Press [CLEAR] once or twice.

   On a line with text on the Home screen, [CLEAR] clears the text from the line.

   On a blank line on the Home screen, [CLEAR] clears the text from the entire screen.

3. Press **500** [( ] **1** [+] **0.0475** [÷] **12** [ )] [^] [( ] **12** [×] **20** [ )] [ENTER].
   (See Fig. 2.5.)

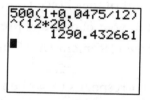

Figure 2.5

4. To display the results in a format more appropriate for calculations involving money,

   a. Press [MODE] to display the MODE screen.

   b. Press [▼] [▶] [▶] [▶] to position the cursor over the 2.

   c. Press [ENTER].

The numerical display format is changed to two fixed decimal places (see Fig. 2.6).

(a)   (b)

Figure 2.6 The Mode screen on the (a) TI-82 and (b) TI-83.

5. Press [2nd] [QUIT] to return to the Home screen.
6. Press [ENTER] to display the result in the two-decimal-place format (see Fig. 2.7).

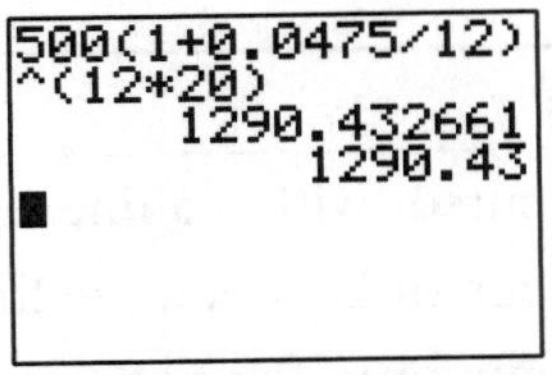

```
500(1+0.0475/12)
^(12*20)
          1290.432661
               1290.43
■
```

Figure 2.7

Our next guess should be quite a bit less than 20 years, say 14 years. In this case, do the following:

1. To edit the old expression, press [2nd] [ENTRY] [◄] [◄] [◄] **14.**
2. Evaluate the edited version by pressing [ENTER] (see Fig. 2.8).

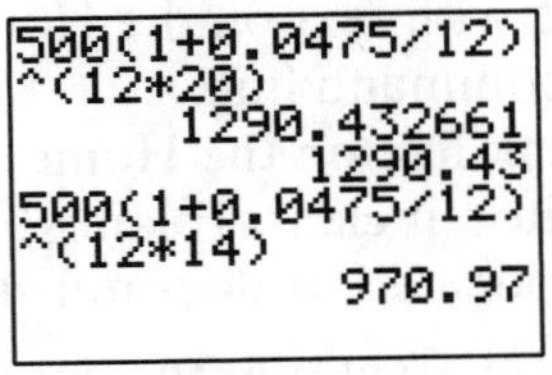

```
500(1+0.0475/12)
^(12*20)
          1290.432661
               1290.43
500(1+0.0475/12)
^(12*14)
                970.97
```

Figure 2.8

3. To change the number of years to 14.5, press

[2nd] [ENTRY] [◄] [·] 5 [ENTER].

Notice that the final parenthesis can be left off and that all three results can be seen on the screen (see Fig. 2.9).

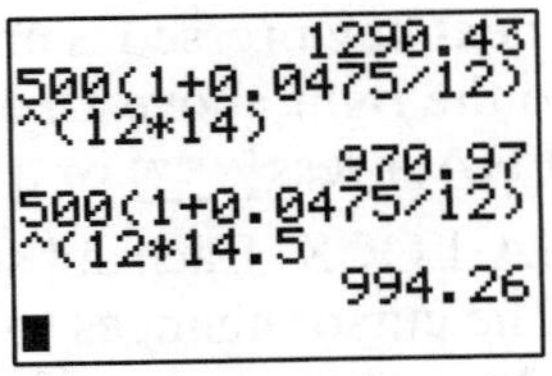

```
               1290.43
500(1+0.0475/12)
^(12*14)
                970.97
500(1+0.0475/12)
^(12*14.5
                994.26
■
```

Figure 2.9

Continue this guess-and-check procedure until you obtain the accuracy you desire. Press [2nd] [ENTRY] several times to observe how the Last Entry Stack has stored several prior entries.

Display Cursors.   There are four types of display cursors. Each of these cursors indicates what will happen when you press the next key (see Table 2.1).

Table 2.1 Display cursors.

Entry cursor	Solid blinking rectangle	The next keystroke is entered at the cursor; it overwrites any character.
INS (insert) cursor	Blinking underline	The next keystroke is inserted in front of the cursor location.
2nd cursor	Blinking ↑	The next keystroke is a 2nd operation.
ALPHA cursor	Blinking A	The next keystroke is an alphabetic character. The SOLVE command may be executed on the TI-83.

Using the Edit Keys. The Edit keys help you make effective use of your calculator. Study Table 2.2.

Table 2.2 Edit keys.

Key	Comments
◄ or ►	Moves the cursor within a line. These keys repeat.
▲ or ▼	Moves the cursor between the lines. These keys repeat.
2nd ◄	Moves the cursor to the beginning of the expression. Can be used for fast-tracing on the Graph screen.
2nd ►	Moves the cursor to the end of the expression. Can be used for fast-tracing on the Graph screen.
ENTER	Evaluates an expression or executes an instruction. This key acts as a Pause key when graphing, press it a second time to resume graphing.
CLEAR	• On a line with text on the Home screen, this key clears (blanks) the current command line. • On a blank line on the Home screen, it clears the screen. • In an editor, it clears (blanks) the expression or value on which the cursor is located. It does not store zero as the value.
DEL	Deletes the character at the cursor. This key repeats.
2nd [INS]	Inserts characters at the underline cursor. To end the insertion, press 2nd [INS] or a cursor-movement key.
2nd	Means the next key pressed is a 2nd operation (the color-coded operation to the left above a key). The cursor changes to an ↑. To cancel 2nd, press 2nd again.
ALPHA	Means the next key pressed is an ALPHA character (the color-coded character to the right above a key). The cursor changes to an A. To cancel ALPHA, press ALPHA or a cursor-movement key.
2nd [A-LOCK]	Sets ALPHA-LOCK. Each subsequent key press is an ALPHA character. The cursor changes to an A. To cancel ALPHA-LOCK, press ALPHA Note that prompts for names automatically set the keyboard in ALPHA-LOCK.
X,T,θ	Allows you to enter an X in Function (Func) mode, a T in Parametric (Par) mode, or a θ in Polar (Pol) mode without pressing ALPHA first. Additionally on the TI-83, the key X,T,θ,n allows you to enter an n in Sequence (Seq) mode.

2.2.5 Scientific Notation and the Answer Key

Example 2 illustrates a geometric progression—a sequence of numbers that grows by a constant factor—while demonstrating some important features of your calculator.

Example 2 Generating a Geometric Sequence

Problem Display the first few terms of the sequence that begins with 1.7×10‹ and grows by a factor of 100.

Solution To generate the sequence, do the following:

1. Return your calculator to Floating Point Numerical Display (Float) mode by pressing MODE ▼ ENTER.

2. Press [2nd] [QUIT] to return to the Home screen.

3. Clear the Home screen by pressing [CLEAR] [CLEAR].

4. To enter 1.7*10< onto the Home screen, press **1.7** [2nd] [EE] **3** [ENTER].

Notice that entering the number in scientific notation did not cause the result to be displayed in scientific notation (see Fig. 2.10).

5. Press [×] **100.**

As soon as you press [×], 'Ans *' is displayed on the screen. **Ans** is a variable that contains the last calculated result (see Fig. 2.11).

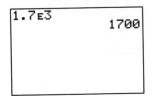

| Figure 2.10 | Figure 2.11 |

6. Press [ENTER] four times.

Each time you press [ENTER], the previous answer is multiplied by 100 and Ans is updated. Notice that the displayed values automatically change to scientific notation after the third iteration (see Fig. 2.12).

7. Press [ENTER] twice to see the geometric progression continue (see Fig. 2.13).

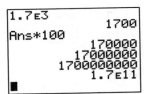 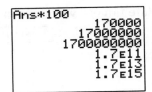

| Figure 2.12 | Figure 2.13 |

2.2.6   Other Computation Features and Menus

Clear the Home screen and then try the following calculations.

1. **Integer Arithmetic**

   To calculate –2–(–3)+(–4)*5, press

   [(–)] **2** [–] [(–)] **3** [+] [(–)] **4** [×] **5** [ENTER].

2. **Rational-number arithmetic**

   To add the fractions $\frac{1}{3}$ and $\frac{4}{7}$, press

   1 [÷] **3** [+] **4** [÷] **7** [MATH] [1: Frac] [ENTER].

3. **Real-number arithmetic**

   To approximate the principal square root of 10, press

   - on the TI-82 [2nd] [√] [( ] **10** [ )] [ENTER].
   - on the TI-83 [2nd] [√] **10** [ )] [ENTER].

   (See Fig. 2.14.)

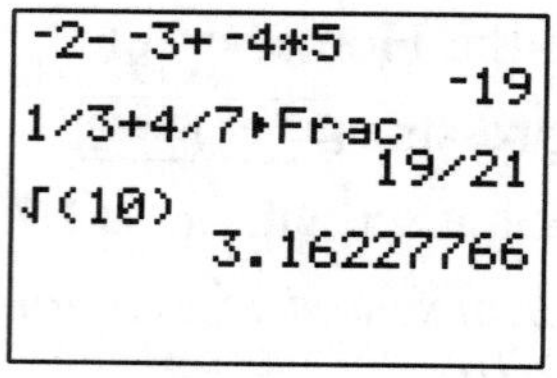

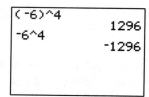

Figure 2.14

4. **Order of operations**

To show that exponents take precedence over negation, and thus $(-6)^4 \neq -6^4$, press

CLEAR ((−) 6) ^ 4 ENTER.

Then press

(−) 6 ^ 4 ENTER.

and compare the results (see Fig. 2.15).

```
(-6)^4
              1296
-6^4
             -1296
```

Figure 2.15

5. **Trig and angle computation**

To calculate tan 60° without switching to Degree mode, press

CLEAR TAN 60 2nd [ANGLE] [1: °] ENTER.

Then press

2nd [√] 3 ENTER.

and compare the results. Re-enter these expressions adding parentheses as needed to match Figure 2.16

6. **Roots**

To evaluate $\sqrt[5]{-16807}$, press either

CLEAR 5 MATH [5: $\sqrt{}$] (−) 16807 ENTER.

or

((−) 16807) ^ (1 ÷ 5) ENTER.

(See Fig. 2.17).

7. **Greatest integer function**

To determine the greatest integer less than or equal to −4.916, press

- on the TI-82 MATH ▶ [4 : int] (−) **4.916** ENTER, or
- on the TI-83 MATH ▶ [5 : int] (−) **4.916** ENTER.

Add parentheses if you wish to match Figure 2.18.

8. **Factorial**

To evaluate $10! = 10 \cdot 9 \cdot 8 \cdot 7 \cdot 6 \cdot 5 \cdot 4 \cdot 3 \cdot 2 \cdot 1$, press

10 MATH ◀ [4 : !] ENTER.

(See Fig. 2.18)

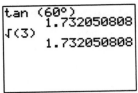

Figure 2.16

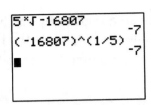

Figure 2.17

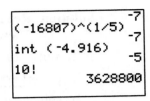

Figure 2.18

2.2.7 Computing with Lists

Set the display format to five fixed decimal places as follows:

1. Press [MODE].
2. Press [▼] and then [▶] six times.
3. Press [ENTER].
4. Return to the Home screen by pressing [2nd] [QUIT] .
5. Clear the Home Screen by pressing [CLEAR].

Patterns in logarithmic outputs

Refer to Figure 2.19 as you proceed through these steps:

1. To enter log(2/), press

[LOG] [( ]† 2 [∧] 1 [ )] [ENTER].

†*This first parenthesis automatically appears on the TI-83.*

2. To enter log(2), press

[2nd] [ENTRY] [◄] [◄] 2 [ENTER].

3. To enter log(2‹), press

[2nd] [ENTRY] [◄] [◄] 3 [ENTER].

See Figure 2.19. Do you see the pattern? A rule of logarithms states that for positive numbers x, $\log(x^n) = n \log(x)$. To see the pattern in a different way.

1. Press [LOG] [2nd] [{] 2 [,] 4 [,] 8 [2nd] [}] [ENTER], *adding parentheses if needed.*
2. Press and hold [▶] to see the third item in the "list." (See Fig. 2.20)

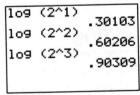

Figure 2.19

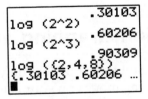

Figure 2.20

The curly braces { } are used to enclose an ordered set of numbers, or **list.** List notation looks just like set notation, but you can add, subtract, multiply, and divide lists, whereas you operate on sets differently, using operations such as union and intersection. Your calculator manual has a chapter on lists. You also can learn about lists through experimentation; try using them in various ways and observe the results.

2.2.8 Using Variables

Example 3 Finding the Height of a Triangle

Problem A triangle encloses an area of 75 cm   and has a base of 11 cm. What is its height?

Solution Recall that the area is given by one half the base times the height: $A=(1/2)bh$. Therefore to find the height, do the following:

1. To put your calculator in Floating Point mode,
   a. press [MODE] and
   b. select the Float option.
2. Return to and clear the Home screen.
3. To store the value 11 as the variable B, press

    11 [STO▸] [ALPHA] **B** [ENTER].

4. Because one-half the base is about 5, the height should be about 15. Therefore press

   • on the TI-82,

    15 [STO▸] [ALPHA] **H** [2nd] [:] [( ] **1** [÷] **2** [ )] [2nd] [A-LOCK] **B H** [ENTER].

   • on the TI-83,

    15 [STO▸] [ALPHA] **H** [ALPHA] [:] [( ] **1** [÷] **2** [ )] [2nd] [A-LOCK] **B H** [ENTER].

   (See Fig. 2.21.)

5. Our guess was too big, so enter

    [2nd] [ENTRY] [▲] **14** [ENTER].

   (See Fig. 2.22.)

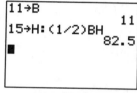

Figure 2.21

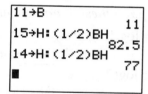

Figure 2.22

The next guess would be between 13 and 14 and would require inserting extra digits for the number being stored in H (press [2nd] [INS] at the appropriate location). Continue the guess-and-check process to practice using the editing features of your calculator and to find the height with an error of no more than 0.01.

2.3 Function Graphing and Table Building

Graphing and table building on your calculator involve the top row of keys. There are four graphing modes on your calculator: Function, Parametric, Polar, and Sequence. Each has a corresponding table-building mode. Thus changing the setting on the fourth line of the Mode screen affects both graphing and table building (see Fig. 2.23).

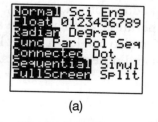

(a)

(b)

Figure 2.23 The Mode screen on the (a) TI-82 and (b) TI-83.

For this section, be sure your calculator is in Function mode (Func). In Section 2.4 we explore the Parametric and Polar modes. The remainder of this section is built around various calculator methods for solving equations, using the example

$$\cos x = \tan x \text{ for } 0 \le x \le 1.$$

2.3.1   Method A: Graphing Each Side and Zooming In

1. Enter each side of the equation as a function on the Y=screen by pressing

$\boxed{\text{Y=}}$ $\boxed{\text{COS}}$ $\boxed{\text{X,T,}\theta}$ $\boxed{\text{ENTER}}$ $\boxed{\text{TAN}}$ $\boxed{\text{X,T,}\theta}$ $\boxed{\text{ENTER}}$.

Insert parentheses if you wish to match Figure 2.24.

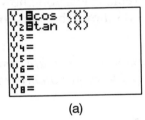   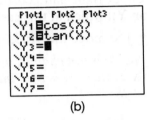

(a)	(b)

Figure 2.24 The Y=screen on the (a) TI-82 and (b) TI-83.

2. Press $\boxed{\text{ZOOM}}$ [4 : ZDecimal].

Watch as the curves are graphed in sequence. The vertical lines are pseudoasymptotes of y=tan x. The calculator is actually connecting points that are off the screen (see Fig. 2.25).

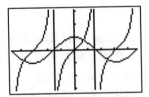

Figure 2.25

3. Press $\boxed{\text{WINDOW}}$ to see what portion of the plane is being used for graphing. The viewing rectangle, or window, being used is [Xmin, Xmax] by [Ymin, Ymax], in this case [−4.7, 4.7] by [−3.1, 3.1]. Because Xscl=1 and Yscl=1, the tick marks on each axis are one unit apart (see Fig. 2.26). The TI-83 has an extra line on the Window screen to set the resolution. For our purposes, keep Xres=1.

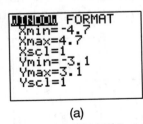   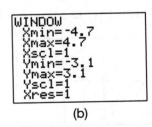

(a)	(b)

Figure 2.26 The Window editor screen on the (a) TI-82 and (b) TI-83.

4. Press $\boxed{\text{TRACE}}$

Observe the coordinate readout at the bottom of the screen as you press and release $\boxed{\blacktriangleright}$ repeatedly. Stop when x=0.7. The graphs appear to intersect at x=0.7; actually this is a rough approximation of the solution we seek for cos x=tan x for $0 \le x \le 1$ (see Fig. 2.27).

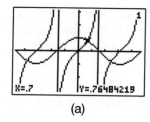
(a)

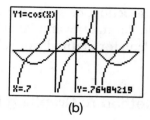
(b)

Figure 2.27 Tracing on the (a) TI-82 and (b) TI-83.

Now you can probably see why the fourth ZOOM feature is called Zoom Decimal (ZDecimal). It adjusted the viewing window to give a nice *decimal* readout. Notice the 1 in the upper right-hand corner of the TI-82 screen. It lets you know that you are tracing on Y_i, which in this case is cos x. The TI-83 shows the equation.

5. Press $\boxed{\blacktriangledown}$ to move the Trace cursor to Y™.

The x value does not change, but the y value does, because you are now tracing on Y™=tan x. Notice the screen indicator has changed to show you are tracing on Y™ (see Fig. 2.28).

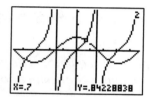

Figure 2.28 TI-82 version

6. Press $\boxed{\text{GRAPH}}$.

The Trace cursor, the coordinate readout, and the number in the upper right-hand corner of the screen all disappear and only the graph itself is displayed (see Fig. 2.29).

7. Press any of the cursor-movement keys. You now are using a free-moving cursor that is not confined to either of the graphs. Notice that this cursor looks different from the Trace cursor.

8. Experiment with all four cursor-movement keys.

Watch the coordinate readout change. Move to the point (0.7, 0.8). Notice $y = 0.8$ is not the value of either function at $x = 0.7$, it is just the y-coordinate of a dot (pixel) on the graphing screen (see Fig. 2.30). The coordinates (0.7, 0.8) are the *screen coordinates* of the pixel. Notice that the free-moving cursor yields a nice decimal readout for both x and y. This is because we used Zoom Decimal to set the viewing window.

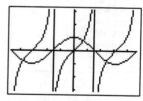
Figure 2.29

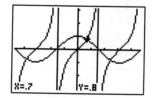
Figure 2.30

Using ZOOM Box.   This option lets you use the cursor to select opposite corners of a "box" to define a new viewing window. Continuing the example from above, do the following:

1. Press [ZOOM] [1 : Box]. Then move the cursor to (0,0). (See Fig. 2.31.)

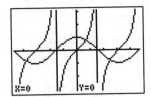

Figure 2.31

2. To select a new viewing window of [0, 1] by [0, 1.2], which will limit *x* so that

$$0 \le x \le 1,$$

   a. press [ENTER] to select the point (0, 0) as one corner of the new viewing window and

   b. use the cursor-movement keys to move to the opposite corner (1, 1.2). (See Fig. 2.32.)

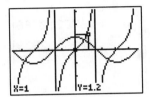

Figure 2.32

3. To select (1, 1.2) as the opposite corner of the new viewing window, press

          [ENTER].

The graphs of the two functions will be drawn in the new viewing window (see Fig. 2.33).

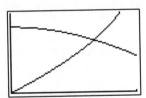

Figure 2.33

4. To remove the cursor and coordinates from the screen, press [GRAPH].

5. To verify that the new viewing rectangle is [0,1] by [0, 1.2], press [WINDOW].

Notice that Xscl and Yscl are still both equal to one. The Zoom Box option does not change the scale settings (see Fig. 2.34).

6. To approximate the solution as x≠0.6702,

   a. press [TRACE] and

   b. use the cursor-movement keys to move to the point of intersection (see Fig. 2.35).

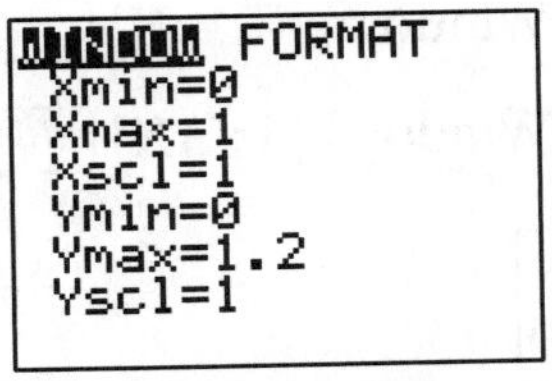

WINDOW FORMAT
Xmin=0
Xmax=1
Xscl=1
Ymin=0
Ymax=1.2
Yscl=1

Figure 2.34 TI-82 version

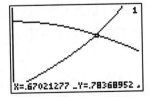

Figure 2.35 TI-82 version

Finding an error bound.   Next, using the approximate solution we found in number 6 above, we want to find the error bound for *x*, as follows:

1. To return to and clear the Home screen, press [2nd] [QUIT] [CLEAR].

2. To see the approximate solution, press ([X,T,θ]) [ENTER].

3. Press

   - on the TI-82 [VARS] [1 : Window] [7 : ΔX] [ENTER] or
   - on the TI-83 [VARS] [1 : Window] [8 : ΔX] [ENTER].

The value of Δx is the horizontal distance between consecutive pixels in the current viewing window, which in this case is about 0.011. This is an error bound for x. Our approximate solution 0.6702, has an error of at most 0.011.

We need to pick Xmin and Xmax so that they are closer together to decrease this error bound (see Fig. 2.36).

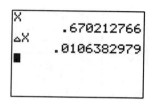

Figure 2.36

Do the following:

1. To enter the smaller window of [0.5, 0.8] by [0.6, 1.0], press [WINDOW], followed on the TI-82 by [▼]; then press

   0.5 [ENTER] **0.8** [ENTER] **0.1** [ENTER] **0.6** [ENTER] **1** [ENTER] **0.1** [ENTER].

   (See Fig. 2.37)

2. To move to the point of intersection—approximately (0.666, 0.786), press

   [TRACE]

   and then after the graph is drawn use the cursor-movement keys (see Fig. 2.38).

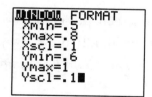

Figure 2.37 TI-82 version

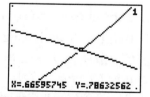

Figure 2.38 TI-82 version.

3. To display the previous approximation and error bound along with the new and improved approximation and error bound (see Fig. 2.39), press

   - on the TI-82 [2nd] [QUIT] [X,T,θ] [ENTER] [VARS] [1 : Window] [7 : ΔX] [ENTER].
   - on the TI-83 [2nd] [QUIT] [X,T,θ] [ENTER] [VARS] [1 : Window] [8 : ΔX] [ENTER].

Figure 2.39

4. Evaluate cos *x* and tan *x* on your calculator. You should see the cos *x* and tan *x* are nearly, but not exactly, equal when $x = 0.6659$»(see Fig. 2.40).

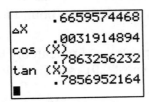

Figure 2.40

2.3.2   Method B: Table Building

The Y=screen is used to enter functions for both graphing and table building. To build a table, do as follows:

1. Press [Y=] to check that Y₁=cos *x* and Y₂=tan *x* (see Fig. 2.41).

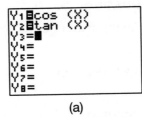
(a)

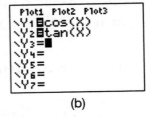
(b)

Figure 2.41 The Y= screen on the (a) TI-82 and (b) TI-83.

2. To reveal the Table Setup screen, press [2nd] [TBLSET].

3. Press **0** [ENTER] **0.1** [ENTER] and ensure the Auto option is selected for both the independent variable (*x*) and the dependent variable (*y*) (see Fig. 2.42).

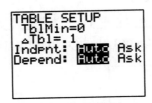

Figure 2.42

4. Press [2nd] [TABLE] and notice that the first *x*-value is the TblMin (=0) and that the increment from one row to the next in the *x* column is Δ Tbl (=0.1) (see Fig. 2.43).

5. Press [▼] repeatedly to move down the *x* column of the table to 0.7. Notice that the solution lies between $x = 0.6$ and $x = 0.7$ (see Fig. 2.44).

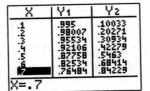

Figure 2.43   **Figure 2.44**

Use the cursor-movement keys to move around the table and explore. Pay attention to the readout at the bottom of the screen as you move to different "cells" in the table.

6. Press

The value of Δ Tbl will serve as the error bound for table building, just as Δx did for graphing (see Fig. 2.45).

7. Press [2nd] [TABLE] and then press [▼] repeatedly until you reach $x = 0.67$. This is a solution with an error of at most 0.01 (see Fig. 2.46).

```
TABLE SETUP
 TblMin=.6
 ΔTbl=.01
Indpnt: Auto Ask
Depend: Auto Ask
```

Figure 2.45

```
 X  │ Y₁    │ Y₂
.61 │.81965 │.69892
.62 │.81388 │.71391
.63 │.80803 │.72911
.64 │.8021  │.74454
.65 │.79608 │.7602
.66 │.78999 │.7761
    │.78382 │.79225
X=.67
```

Figure 2.46

2.3.3 Method C: Solving an Equivalent Equation

To solve cos x=tan x for $0 \le x \le 1$, you can solve the equivalent equation

$$\cos x\text{-}\tan x=0$$

for the same interval. To do this on the TI-82, follow these steps:

1. Press

[Y=] [▼] [▼] [2nd] [Y-VARS]† [1 : Function»] [1 : Y₁] [—] [2nd]
[Y-VARS]† [1 : Function»] [2 : Y₂] [ENTER]

†On the TI-83, use [VARS] [▶] in place of [2nd] [Y-VARS].
(See Fig. 2.47).

2. To deselect Y₁ and Y™, press

[▲] [▲] [◀] [ENTER] [▲] [ENTER].

Now only Y£ should have its equals sign highlighted (see Fig. 2.48).

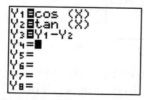

Figure 2.47 TI-82 version.

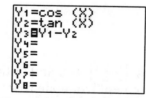

Figure 2.48 TI-82 version.

3. To see the graph of y=cos x-tan x in a "friendly" viewing window, press
[ZOOM] [4 : ZDecimal]; and after the graph is drawn, press

[TRACE] [2nd] [▶] [▶] [▶].

Notice [2nd] [▶] *moves the cursor five pixels to the right for fast tracing (see Fig. 2.49).*

4. To enter the Zoom Factors screen, press

[ZOOM] [▶] [4 : SetFactors»]

and enter 10 as both the horizontal and the vertical magnification factor by pressing

10 [ENTER] **10** [ENTER].

(See Fig 2.50.)

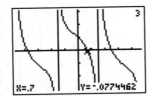

Figure 2.49 TI-82 version.

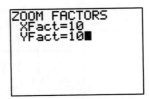

Figure 2.50

5. To center your zoom-in at the point $(x, y) = (0.7, 0)$, press

$$\boxed{\text{ZOOM}} \; [2 : \text{ZoomIn}]$$

and move the cursor to $(0.7, 0)$. (See Fig. 2.51.)

Then press $\boxed{\text{ENTER}}$ to zoom in.

6. After the graph is redrawn, you can obtain the same approximation that was found by Method B by pressing

$$\boxed{\text{TRACE}} \; \boxed{\blacktriangleleft} \; \boxed{\blacktriangleleft} \; \boxed{\blacktriangleleft}.$$

Check the value of Δx; it is the same as the Δ Tbl in method B! (See Fig. 2.52.)

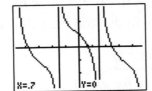

Figure 2.51 TI-82 version.

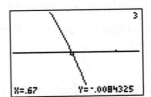

Figure 2.52

2.3.4   Other Equation-Solving Methods

Traditional algebra and trigonometry can be used to determine the exact solution of equation 1.

$$x = \sin^{-1}\frac{-1 + \sqrt{5}}{2}$$

Do the following:

1. To evaluate this expression on your calculator, enter it as shown in Figure 2.53.

You obtain an approximation that is accurate to 10 decimal places. It should be consistent with those found by Methods A, B, and C, and it is (see Fig. 2.53).

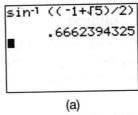

(a)

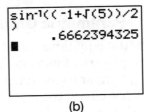

(b)

Figure 2.53 An arcsin computation on the (a) T1-82 and (b) T1-83

2. Set up your Y=screen as you did for Method C. Then, to obtain a graph, press

$$\boxed{\text{ZOOM}} \; [4 : \text{ZDecimal}].$$

3. Press $\boxed{\text{2nd}} \; \boxed{\text{CALC}} \; [2 : \text{root}].$ (On the T1-83, the word "zero" appears rather than "root.")
This should yield a prompt requesting a Lower Bound or Left Bound (see Fig. 2.54).

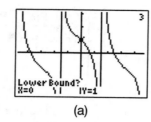 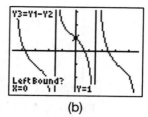

(a)   (b)

Figure 2.54 (a) Root finder on the T1-82, (b) zero finder on the T1-83.

4. Because we are seeking a solution for $0 \le x \le 1$, the lower bound should be $x = 0$; so press [ENTER].

5. To move the cursor to $x = 1$, press

followed by [ENTER] to enter it as the upper bound.

6. Move the Trace cursor to $x=0.7$ and enter it as your guess by pressing

[◄] [◄] [◄] [ENTER].

The calculator should yield a root value of $x = 0.66623943$ (see Fig. 2.55).

7. To compare the value found using the root finder and the value found in Part 1 above, press

[X,T,θ] [ENTER].

They match perfectly to 10 decimal places! (See fig. 2.56.)

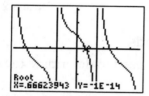   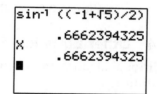

Figure 2.55 TI-82 version.   **Figure 2.56** TI-82 version.

There are many other ways to solve equations on your calculator. Feel free to explore them.

2.4 Other Graphing and Table Building

2.4.1 Parametric Graphing and Table Building

Parametric equations are ideal tools for representing and solving problems in geometry and the physics of motion. Your calculator has a built-in parametric graphing utility. This utility is similar to the function graphing utility and is almost as easy to use. To graph a parametric curve, you

- select the parametric (Par) mode on the Mode screen.
- type the desired equations in the Y= screen,
- set the intervals for t, x, and y using the Window screen, and
- press [GRAPH].

Parametric equations are written in the form:

$$x = f(t) \text{ and } y = g(t).$$

In this setting *t* is called a parameter; however, *t* actually is an independent variable, not a parameter in the sense that *m* and *b* are parameters in the equation $y = mx + b$. Unlike the independent variable *x* we are used to in Function-graphing mode, the parameter *t* is not a plotted, visible coordinate; it is hidden from view when we look at a parametric curve. When we use the TRACE feature, we see a readout of the parameter *t* and the coordinates *x* and *y*, which are the dependent variables of the parametric representation.

Example 4 Graphing a Parametric Curve

Problem Graph the curve represented by the following parametric equations:
$$x = t^2 \text{ and } y = t - 1 \text{ for } -2 \le t \le 2.$$

Solution To solve this problem, follow these steps:

1. Press ⌈MODE⌉ to enter the Mode screen and

    a. select Parametric Graphing (Par) and

    b. choose the default (leftmost) settings for the other mode settings.

2. Because we are in Parametric mode, pressing ⌈X,T,θ⌉ will yield the letter *t*. To enter the given parametric equations, press

    ⌈Y=⌉ ⌈X,T,θ⌉ ⌈x^2⌉ ⌈ENTER⌉ ⌈X,T,θ⌉ ⌈—⌉ 1 ⌈ENTER⌉.

The screen should look like Figure 2.57.

(a)   (b)

Figure 2.57 The Y= screen on the (a) T1-82 and (b) T1-83.

3. Press ⌈WINDOW⌉ and then set the Window screen as shown in Figure 2.58. (Note that you won't be able to see the entire screen at once because it has too many lines.)

```
WINDOW FORMAT
 Tmin=-2
 Tmax=2
 Tstep=.1
 Xmin=-4.7
 Xmax=4.7
 Xscl=1
 Ymin=-3.1
 Ymax=3.1
 Yscl=1
```

Figure 2.58 Facsimile of the Window screen.

The *t* step on the Parametric Window screen is the change between the successive *t*-values that the calculator uses to compute and plot (x, y) pairs. In this case, the *t* step of 0.1 will yield 40 steps from the *t* Min of –2 to the *t* Max of 2. Thus 41 points will be calculated and plotted, with the points corresponding to
$$t = -2.0, -1.9, -1.8, -1.7, \ldots, 1.9, 2.0.$$

Table 2.3 shows the numerical relationship between the parameter *t* and the coordinates *x* and *y* for some of the points to be plotted.

The last two columns of Table 2.3 determine the (x, y) coordinate pairs to be plotted. The values of the parameter *t* will not appear on the graph.

You can create a table like Table 2.3 on your calculator as follows:

1. Press $\boxed{\text{2nd}}$ $\boxed{\text{TBLSET}}$ $\boxed{(-)}$ **2** $\boxed{\text{ENTER}}$ **0.1** $\boxed{\text{ENTER}}$. (See Fig. 2.59.)
2. Then press $\boxed{\text{2nd}}$ $\boxed{\text{TABLE}}$. (See Fig. 2.60.)

Table 2.3 Table of Parameter and Coordinate Values

t	$x=t^2$	$y=t-1$
−2.0	4.00	−3.0
−1.9	3.61	−2.9
−1.8	3.24	−2.8
−1.7	2.89	−2.7
.	.	.
.	.	.
.	.	.
1.9	3.61	0.9
2.0	4.00	1.0

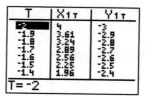

Figure 2.59

Figure 2.60

To obtain the graph corresponding to Table 2.3 and Figure 2.60, do the following:

1. Press $\boxed{\text{GRAPH}}$ to yield the plot shown in Figure 2.61.

Because the calculator is in Connected mode, the plotted points in Figure 2.61 are connected by the line segments.

2. To display only the 41 plotted points, choose the Dot mode from the Mode screen and press $\boxed{\text{GRAPH}}$ again (see Fig. 2.62).

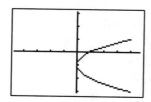

Figure 2.61

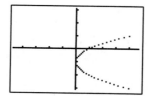

Figure 2.62

Return to Connected mode and use the TRACE feature and the left and right cursor-movement keys to explore the graph numerically. Notice that the values of the parameter t and the x- and y-coordinates are all shown on the screen (see Fig. 2.63 and 2.64). Can you find the six points that correspond to the completed rows of Table 2.3?

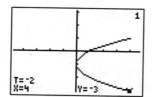

Figure 2.63 TI-82 version.

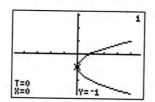

Figure 2.64 TI-82 version.

2.4.2   Polar Equation Graphing

The Polar Equation graphing mode is similar to the other graphing modes.

Example 5   Graphing Two Equations Simultaneously

Problem   Graph $r = 9 \sin 5\theta$ and $r = 9$.
Solution

1. Press [MODE] (see Fig. 2.65) and

   a. select Polar (Pol) mode and Simultaneous (Simul) mode and

   b. choose the defaults for the other modes.

2. Press [Y=] to display the Polar Equation screen.

3. To define the two desired equations, press

$$9 \; [\text{SIN}] \; 5 \; [\text{X,T,}\theta] \; [\text{ENTER}] \; 9 \; [\text{ENTER}].$$

   (See Fig. 2.66.)

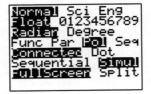

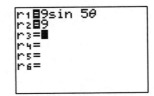

Figure 2.65 TI-82 version.   **Figure 2.66** TI-82 version.

4. Press [ZOOM] [6 : ZStandard].

The graph of r = 9 is a circle of radius 9 centered at the pole. The circle circumscribes the five-petaled rose curve r = 9 sin 5θ (see Fig. 2.67).

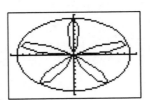

Figure 2.67

5. Set θmax $= \pi$ in the Window screen.

6. To "square up" the window, press

$$[\text{ZOOM}] \; [5 : \text{ZSquare}].$$

The entire rose curve is plotted using the interval $0 \le \theta \le \pi$. Press [TRACE] and explore the two curves (see Fig. 2.68).

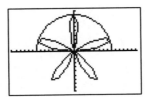

Figure 2.68

CHAPTER

3

The Casio CFX-9850G Graphing Calculator

3.1 Preliminaries

The Casio CFX-9850G is a graphing calculator with the added capability of using color. In this chapter many of its features will be introduced. Some will incorporate color and others will not, as color is only one of its assets. In order to ease the process of reading the material, a boxed notation will be used. When referring to the primary function of a key, the single function name written on the key will be in the box; when referring to a secondary (or alpha) function of a key, the box will have the function name of the key followed by a colon and the name of the function needed, both contained in brackets. For example, to "insert", the instructions would be "press [SHIFT][[DEL]:INS]". Bold italics will be used to indicate a Menu such as "press [MENU] to activate the ***Main Menu*** screen."

3.1.1 Keyboard

The keys on the calculator are color coded to allow each key to be used for three different commands. Primary key functions are printed on the key in white, secondary key functions are printed in yellow, and alpha key functions are in orange red. For example, if e^x is needed, press [SHIFT][[LN]:e^x] or, if the symbol for theta is needed, press [ALPHA][[∧]:θ].

The six keys labeled F1 through F6 at the top of the keyboard will be referred to as "soft menu keys". The soft menu keys control user-activated commands located on the calculator screen just above the keys. The cluster of four arrow keys located at the upper right of the keyboard will be referred to as cursor keys or **replay keys.**

3.1.2 Menus

The Casio CFX-9850G is menu-driven with fourteen menu choices. The ***Main Menu*** screen, shown below, is activated when the calculator is turned on. Any of the fourteen

Figure 3.1 Main Menu

sub-menus can be activated either by pressing the number on the calculator corresponding to the number displayed in the lower right corner of the menu block or by using the cursor arrows to highlight the needed menu, followed by pressing [EXE].

Each of the fourteen menus on the **Main Menu** screen has its own set-up screen which is activated by pressing [SHIFT] followed by [[MENU]:SET UP] after getting into the desired menu. As a reference, an example of two of the fourteen set-up screens is illustrated. An arrow above the soft menu key [F6] indicates that there are more items on the set-up screen to be seen.

Figure 3.2 Run Menu

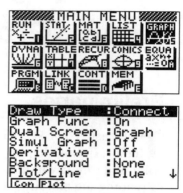

Figure 3.3 Graph Menu

3.1.3 Color Feature

Color is the new feature of the Casio series of calculators. It is an excellent feature to clarify a graph's position in relation to another graph as well as providing a shading tool. As a default, inequality graphs are shaded in orange, integral graphs (for calculus students) are shaded in blue. Since color is used with the **Graph** and **Stat Modes,** those are the sections in which color will be addressed more thoroughly.

3.2   Basic Operations

3.2.1 Exiting a Screen

It is always frustrating to get into a menu screen and find that it seems impossible to get out of the operation. To get out of a screen, **always** remember to press [EXIT] until the calculator no longer changes screens; then press [MENU].

3.2.2 Calculating Numerical Expressions

In order to enter numerical expressions, activate the **Run Menu** by highlighting it and pressing the execute key or by pressing the number 1 when the **Main Menu** is displayed. Begin by evaluating the following expressions. Enter each expression followed by [EXE].

$$2(3 + 5)$$

$$\sqrt{4}$$

$$(3 + 5)2$$

- **Receiving Error Messages**

    In evaluating the first two of the three given expressions, notice that the answer for the first was found to be 16 and the answer to the second was found to be 2. However, when attempting to evaluate the third expression, observe that "Syn ERROR" appears at the bottom of the screen. To locate the error, press either the **right** or the **left replay arrows.** By pressing the replay arrow a cursor will blink at the point at which the calculator does not recognize the syntax. In this particular problem, the cursor is blinking on the number 2 indicating that the calculator does not know what to do with this number. The Casio does not recognize a number on the right of a parenthesis without an operational symbol.

- **Editing**

To edit the expression $(3 + 5)2$ with the blinking cursor on the number 2, press [SHIFT] [DEL :INS]. Observe that the blinking cursor over the 2 has changed from solid to open in the middle. This form of the cursor is used to indicate insert mode. Press [×] followed by [EXE] to get the correct result of 16.

Enter the number 235652701 and press [EXE]. To change the 3 in the number to a 4, press the **right replay arrow.** The **right replay arrow** will place the cursor at the far left of the number to indicate it will move to the right for correction. Arrow to the number 3 to be changed, put a 4 in its place, then press [EXE].

Suppose the number 7 should have been another 2. Press the **left replay arrow** to place the cursor at the far right of the last entry, indicating the cursor will move left to make corrections. Arrow to the left until the 7 is blinking, change it to a 2, then press [EXE].

3.2.3   Using the Deep Stack

A useful feature of the Casio 9850G is the deep stack. Assuming that the calculator has not been turned off since the first calculations were entered in section 3.2.2, press [AC/ON] one time followed by the **up replay key.** The last changed entry, 245652201, will appear on the screen.

Continue to press the **up replay key** until the first entry $2(3 + 5)$ is reached. Any of the previous computational entries may be accessed and edited by using the deep stack feature as long as the **_Run Menu_** was never exited. When at the top of the stack, the **down replay arrow** may be used to return to another entry.

3.2.4   Working with Fractions

Fraction operations are easy to work with by using the [**a%**] key. Enter 2/3 by pressing 2 [**a%**] 3 [EXE]. The result will appear on the screen as 2⌐3. See Figure 3.4.

Figure 3.4 Fraction Operations

To change this result to a decimal press [F↔D]. This key acts as a toggle between the fraction and its decimal equivalent. To see this, press [F↔D] again to return to 2⌐3. The second function of this key acts as a toggle between a mixed number and its improper equivalent. Press 1 [**a%**] 2 [**a%**] 3 [EXE]. This will be shown as 1⌐2⌐3 on the screen. Press [SHIFT] [**a%** :d/c] to get a result of 5⌐3.

Suppose the fractions 1/5 and 7/8 are to be added. Enter 1 [**a%**] 5 [+] 7 [**a%**] 8 [EXE]. The result is given as 1⌐3⌐40. If [SHIFT] [**a%** :d/c] is pressed, the improper fractional equivalent 43⌐40 is given. Now press [F↔D] to see that the decimal equivalent is 1.075. At this point, if [F↔D] is pressed again, 1⌐3⌐40 will be returned; however, if [SHIFT] [**a%** :d/c] is pressed, the result will be the improper form 43⌐40 once again.

3.2.5   Using Complex Numbers

Although the Casio 9850G is not a calculator based on the complex number system, it has the capability to calculate using complex numbers. To perform complex number operations in the **Run Menu** press the options key [OPTN] on the keyboard.

Soft menus are now found at the bottom of the viewing screen. Observe that each of the menu names is solid with the bottom right corner cut off. This indicates that there is another function under the menu.

Figure 3.5 Cut Off Corners   **Figure 3.6** Solid Menu Commands

Press [F3 :CPLX]. Observe that the soft menu commands are now solid (no corners are cut off). This indicates that the menu commands are functions in and of themselves and there is no other command to be found after pressing the key.

To enter the complex number $(3 - 2i)$ and add it to $(2 + 7i)$, press [( ] 3 [—] 2 [[F1]:i] [ )] [+] [( ] 2 [+] 7 [[F1]:i] [ )] [EXE]. (Note that it is not necessary to put parentheses in this expression, but the same two numbers will be edited to perform other complex operations which will need the parentheses.) The answer to this addition problem should be $5 + 5i$. See Figure 3.7. To subtract the same two complex numbers, press the **right (or left) replay arrow,** and cursor to the ' + ' symbol in the problem; change this plus to minus, and press [EXE]. Now the result should be $1 - 9i$. Continue the edit process to multiply (Ans: $20 + 17i$) and divide the two numbers (Ans:-0.1509433962-0.4716981132i) by pressing the replay arrow and moving the cursor until it is over the operation symbol to change. Replace the operation with the multiplication ($\times$) or division ($\div$) symbol.

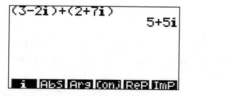

Figure 3.7 Complex Operations

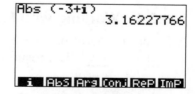

Figure 3.8 Complex Operations

To see other features of the calculator's complex operations, press [F2 :AbS] [( ] [(−)] 3 [+] [F1]:i] [ )] [EXE]. This series of key strokes finds the absolute value (or magnitude) of the complex number $(-3 + i)$ which is seen to be 3.16227766. See Figure 3.8.

The other menu keys, in order from left to right, will display the Argument [Arg] of the complex number, its Conjugate [Conj], its Real Part [ReP] and its Imaginary Part [ImP]. The function command and complex number should be entered in the same way they were entered to find the complex number's absolute value.

3.2.6   Computing with Variables

Suppose that the polynomial $x^2 + x - 5$ is to be evaluated for multiple values of x without using a table. This can be accomplished by storing an initial value for x in its variable location followed by a colon and the polynomial. After pressing [EXE] for the first answer, the **right** or **left replay arrows** may be used to change the stored value of *x* and the expression evaluated again upon pressing [EXE].

For example, enter the following keystrokes and observe the results obtained in the first illustration. Press 1 [→] [X,θ,T] [SHIFT] [[VARS]:PRGM] [[F6]: ▶] [[F5]::] [X,θ,T] [x^2] [+] [X,θ,T] [−] 5 [EXE]. The answer of −3 is displayed. Press the **right arrow replay** key and change the value stored in *x* to 5, then press [EXE]. This time, 25 is the result. If a two or more digit number is required, then remember to press [SHIFT][[DEL]: INS] first before inserting the additional digit.

This procedure can be used to change more than one variable in an expression. Evaluate $A^3 + 2B^2 - 7C$, for various values of *A, B,* and *C.* As initial values, store 3 in *A,* 1 in *B,* and 2 in *C* following each entry by the colon; then enter the expression to be evaluated and press the execute key. Note that [∧] is used to place the exponent, 3, on *A.* Press either the **right** or the **left replay** to change any of the values for *A, B,* and *C,* and after the desired change has been made, press [EXE].

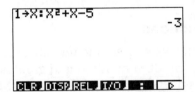

Figure 3.9 Polynomial Evaluation

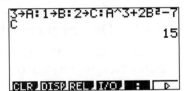

Figure 3.10 Multiple Variables

3.2.7   Computing with Lists

Be sure to create a List under the **List Menu** before operating with lists in the **Run Menu.** If a list is not available for computation, proceed to the **List Menu** section of this chapter where the topics of entering lists are explained.

If lists are entered, press [OPTN] and [[F1]:List] to activate the **LIST** commands. Basic arithmetic operations may be performed using lists. For example, to add **List 1** to **List 2** and place the result in **List 1**, highlight **List 1** using the **replay keys**. Then, simply press [[F1]:List] 1 [+] [[F1]:List] 2 [EXE]. If the lists being added have a different number of entries, a dim error will appear, since in order to perform arithmetic operations on lists, the dimensions must be the same.

Figure 3.11 List Menu

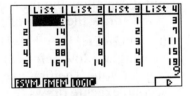

Figure 3.12 List More

Functional operations may be performed on lists while in the **List Menu.** Press [OPTN][[F1]:LIST]. To take the natural log of the elements in **List 1,** highlight **List 1** and press [ln][[F1]:List] 1 [EXE]. If values appear in the list which are not in the domain of the natural log function, "ma ERROR" is displayed.

Other List operations are performed in the **Run Menu** such as determining the dimension of a stored list, its minimum value, its maximum value, its mean, and its median.

3.2.8 Computing Matrices

To add, subtract, and multiply matrices, the ***Run Menu*** must be used. After entering the ***Run Menu,*** press [OPTN] on the keyboard followed by [[F2]:MAT]. If matrices have been entered into the locations A and B using the ***Matrix Menu,*** press [[F1]:Mat] [ALPHA] [[X,θ,T]:A] [+] [[F1]:Mat] [ALPHA] [[LOG]:B] [EXE] to add the matrices. To find any other

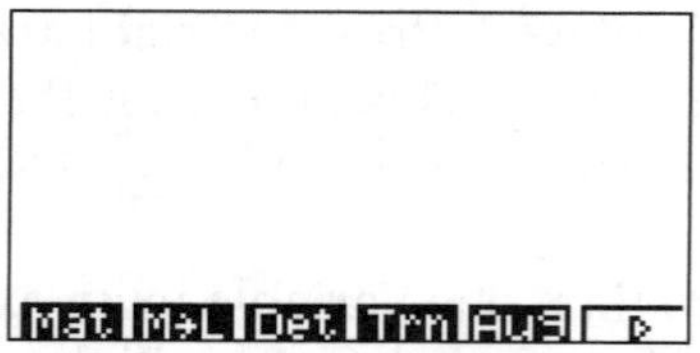

Figure 3.13 Matrix Menu

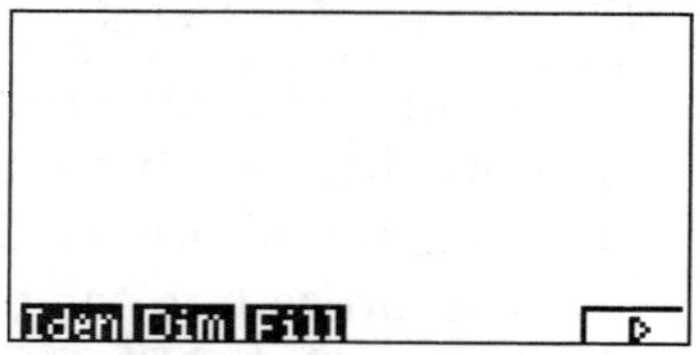

Figure 3.14 Matrix More

matrix property, always remember to insert the word matrix first. For example, to find the determinant of a matrix while in the ***Run Menu,*** under [OPTN][F2]:MAT] press [[F3]:Det] [[F1]:Mat] [ALPHA] [[X,θ,T]:A] [EXE].

3.2.9 Discovering Other Number Functions

Other number functions which are found in the ***Run Menu*** include absolute value, integer part of a number, fractional part of a number, random number, and greatest integer.

To access the number features listed, press [OPTN][F6]: ▶] [[F4]:NUM]. The number concepts are shown as a soft menu. While arrowing through the soft menus for [OPTN], other menu items observed which have not been addressed at this time include CALC, STAT, COLR, HYP, PROB, ANGL, ESYM, PICT, FMEM, and LOGIC. Menus which have not been addressed, but which relate to topics in this manual, will be presented in later sections.

3.3 Graphs

3.3.1 Graphing in the Run Menu

Graphs can be sketched in the ***Run Menu*** in the same way graphs were sketched on the first Casio Graphing Calculator produced. It is not as an efficient way to draw graphs, but it can allow the user to stay in the same menu when working with computations.

To draw the graph of $y = x^2$ while in the ***Run Menu,*** press [SHIFT][F4]:[SKETCH] [[F5]:GRPH] [[F1]:Y=] [X,θ,T] [x^2]. To set the Viewing Window to the "standard" viewing window before drawing the graph, press [SHIFT][[F3]:V-Window] [[F3]:STD] [EXE] [EXE]. (Note: The first execute returns to the screen where the function was entered. The second execute draws the graph.)

It is important to remember that when graphing in the ***Run Menu,*** [[F1]:Cls] must be pressed each time a graph is sketched unless the previous graph is also needed. Otherwise, all previous graphs will appear on the same graph screen as the one presently being sketched. The previous graphs can also be erased by changing the viewing window.

3.3.2 Using the Graph Stack

The graph stack is activated by pressing the number 5 on the ***Main Menu*** screen or by highlighting the fifth square of the menu and pressing [EXE]. There are twenty possible entries of graphs on the stack. When using the graph stack, the "function mode" of the highlighted graph is given at the top of the screen.

A graph in any mode (rectangular, polar, or parametric) and inequality graphs may be entered on the same stack. After entering the functions on the stack, the different modes may be sketched on the same screen or they may be chosen to be sketched alone.

Remember, when changing to a new function mode, the change must be made on a blank line. The mode of the function to be entered on a line cannot be changed when the line is not empty.

- **Entering Equations and Inequalities on the Stack**

To illustrate the versatility of the Casio 9850G graph stack, the following functions will be entered and sketched in various combinations.

(1) $y = x(x - 1)(x + 1)$ (2) $y = \sin 2x$

(3) $r = \sin 2\theta$ (4) $\begin{cases} xt = t^2 \\ yt = t \end{cases}$

(5) $y \geq |x + 1| - 3$ (6) $y \leq -|x + 1| + 3$

(7) $y = [x]$ (8) $y = \text{intg}\,(x)$

Before entering the given equations, delete any previous functions from the stack by highlighting the function to be deleted and pressing [[F2]:DEL] and [[F1]:YES].

The first equation to be entered is **rectangular.** Therefore, press [[F3]:TYPE] [[F1]:Y=]. Then, to enter the first equation press [X,θ,T] [( ] [X,θ,T] [−] 1 [ )] [( ] [X,θ,T] [+] 1 [ )] [EXE]. (The execute command, at the end of the key strokes, places the equation on the stack and highlights the next position on the stack.) If an error is made while entering a function, press the **right replay arrow** with the position to be corrected highlighted. The equation line will be reactivated to allow the correction to be made.

In the second position, enter the next rectangular equation with the key strokes [SIN] 2 [X,θ,T] [EXE].

- **Changing Graph Types on the Stack**

The next equation to be entered is a **polar equation.** Since it is not the same as the rectangular equations entered in Y1 and Y2, the **Graph Type** must be changed before entering it on the stack. While the highlight is on the empty position, Y3, press [[F3]:TYPE] [[F2]: r =] [SIN] 2 [X,θ,T] [EXE].

Equation four is given in the form of **parametric equations.** To enter the set of parametric equations, the **Graph Type** must be changed again. Highlight [[F3]:TYPE] [[F3]:Parm].

Observe that all locations from position four and higher have both XT and YT: i.e., on entry 4, both XT4 and YT4 are found. Next to XT4 enter [X,θ,T] [x²] [EXE] and next to YT4 enter [X,θ,T] [EXE].

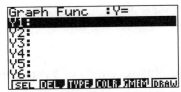

Figure 3.15 Graph Stack

Figure 3.16 Multiple Graph Types

An **inequality** expression is to be entered next, requiring once again that the **Graph Type** must be changed. Highlight the next empty position represented at this point by XT5. Press [[F3]:TYPE] [F6]: ▶ [[F6]:≥]. To access absolute value, press [OPTN] [[F5]:NUM]

[[F1]:AbS]. Continue to enter the expression by pressing [( ] [X,θ,T] [+] 1 [ )] [−] 3 [EXE]. The inequality expression number (6) may now be entered without changing the type, and by following essentially the same instructions for the number (5) inequality. Be careful, however, to put the minus (−) sign in front of the absolute value symbol and use F4 for ≤ instead of F3.

To enter the last two equations, the **Graph Type** must be returned to **rectangular.** Once again, this is accomplished by highlighting the first empty position, Y7, and pressing [[F3]:TYPE] [[F1]:Y =]. The following key strokes will enter graphs (7) and (8). Press [OPTN] [[F5]:NUM] [[F2]:Int] [X,θ,T] [EXE]; [OPTN] [[F5]:NUM] [[F5]:Intg] [X,θ,T] [EXE].

• Selecting a Function's Color

Suppose the graphs of $y = \sin 2x$ and $r = \sin 2\theta$ are to be drawn on the same viewing screen window. In order to visualize the difference between the two graphs, it is decided that the rectangular graph will be sketched in blue, but the polar graph will be sketched in orange.

Use the **replay arrows** to highlight Y2. To select a color for the highlighted graph, press [[F4]:COLR] and choose [[F1]:Blue]. Move the highlight down to r3 and press [[F2]:Orng]. While changing colors, highlight Y7 and change it to green [[F3]:Grn], then highlight Y8 and choose orange [[F2]:Orng].

• Selecting a Function to Be Sketched

Now that all of the functions have been entered on the stack, and colors selected, the equations and inequalities may be chosen to be sketched when needed. Observe that when a function is entered on the stack, there is a colored square over the equal sign opposite the highlight; i.e., if the equation is highlighted, the square over the equal sign is clear; if the equation is not highlighted, the square over the equal sign **is** highlighted. In other words, if the square over the equal sign is the opposite of the highlighted equation then that equation has been selected to be sketched. If the square over the equal sign has the same shading as the highlighted graph's shading then the function will not be drawn. Press [EXIT] until no change is being made on the screen. The stack should be on the screen and the soft menu above [F1] should be **SEL**. This key acts as a toggle for turning the graphs on and off.

Use the **replay arrows** and highlight Y1. Turn this function off by pressing [[F1]:SEL]. Repeat for all functions except Y5 and Y6. If all lines on the stack are turned off except the two inequalities, press [[F6]:DRAW].

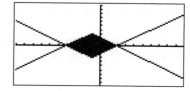

Figure 3.17 Inequalities

3.3.3 Using the Soft Menu Keys

The graph just drawn should look similar to the illustration. If this is not the case the graph's viewing window may be set differently.

• V-Window

To set the viewing window, press [SHIFT] [[F3]:V-Window] if the graph is not visible. If the graph is visible, the same result will occur by simply pressing the function key [F3]. The window can now be changed to any desired setting. The soft menu keys provide three pre-set screens. The [INIT] or initialized window is based on the spacing of the pixels on the Casio calculator, [TRIG] provides a standard window for most trigonometry functions, and [STD] provides a standard viewing window used on most calculators for algebraic functions. If another window is needed, a custom viewing window can be entered by the user.

To enter a user defined viewing window, enter each number followed by [EXE]. Which of the two keys [(−)] or [−] used is not significant in the viewing window format. It should also be noted that the only function of **scale** is to put "tick" marks on the graph screen to indicate divisions.

The V-Window screen is activated with the rectangular graph's settings. To observe the settings for polar and additional settings needed for parametric equations, arrow down to the next screen. On this extension of the V-Window screen, "min" and "max" refer to the values of θ and t and pitch indicates the point change. For example, if 0.5 was entered for pitch in the radian mode, the calculator would plot one point (or pixel) every 0.5 radian.

Set the V-Window to **STD**, [EXIT] and press [[F6]:DRAW]. [EXIT] and use [[F1]:SEL] to unselect Y5 and Y6. Select Y1 and press [[F6]:DRAW].

- **Trace**

With the Y1 function drawn on the screen, activate the trace feature by pressing [F1]. The shift key only needs to be used when the graph screen is not showing.

On the graph screen, the equation of the drawn function is displayed at the top of the screen, and the x and y coordinates of the cursor location are shown at the bottom of the screen while the trace feature is on. Use the **right replay arrow** to move the cursor into view and observe the location indicated. Remember, the trace only addresses the pixels on the screen; therefore, false information could be obtained if looking for particular features of the graph.

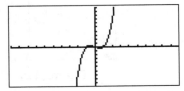

Figure 3.18 Graph of Y1

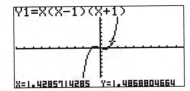

Figure 3.19 Trace of Y1

- **Zoom**

Activate the **Zoom** feature by pressing [F2]. Five soft menus appear at the bottom of the screen with an arrow over [F6] indicating there is more to the menu. Press [F6] and press it again. It is seen that there are two complete soft menu lists for **Zoom.**

Observe, in particular, [[F1]:BOX] and [[F5]:AUTO] on the first menu set and [[F1]:ORIG], [[F2]:SQR], and [[F5]:PRE] on the second menu set. [[F5]:AUTO] sets the V-Window to a zoom screen determined by the calculator, [[F1]:ORG] puts the V-Window to the original screen settings used to sketch the graph, and [[F5]:PRE] returns the V-Window to the setting most recently used (that is, its previous setting). [[F2]:SQR] is useful to make graphs such as circles look like circles. This command allows the "squaring" of the V-Window. Finally, [[F1]:BOX] allows the user to define exactly the region to be enlarged.

To isolate a region using the box command, press [[F1]:BOX] with the graph of Y1 on the screen. When this command is activated, the cursor is initially placed at the origin $(0, 0)$. Using the **replay arrows,** move the cursor approximately to the point $(2, 3)$. Press [EXE] to fix one corner of the box. Observe that the cursor has changed to a fixed " + ". Arrow down and left to approximately $(−2, −3)$. Notice that as the cursor moves, a box is formed. Press [EXE] to zoom in on this region.

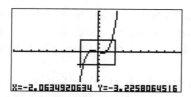

Figure 3.20 Zoom Box

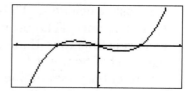

Figure 3.21 Zoom Result

- **Sketch**

   While in the ***Graph Menu,*** the soft menu key [[F4]:Sketch] can be used to draw the inverse of a function as well as vertical and horizontal lines. The commands for drawing a circle, the tangent line to a curve, and the normal line to a curve are also found in this soft menu.

- **G-Solv**

   The graph of Y1 should be on the screen with a V-Window of approximately x-min $= -2$ to x-max $= 2$ and a scale of 1 due to using the Zoom Feature. Enter the function "$y = x$" on the stack in the Y9 location and press [[F6]:DRAW] to overlay its graph over Y1.

   Press [[F5]:G-Solv]. To illustrate the features of **Graph Solve,** press [[F1]:ROOT]. The cursor will appear at the far lower left corner of the screen, and the equation of the function which the cursor is on, Y1, will be displayed at the top of the screen. Press [EXE] to activate the cursor; it will stop on the first root $x = -1$. Now press the **right replay arrow** and the cursor will move to the next root $x = 0$; press the **right replay arrow** again to get to the last root $x = 1$.

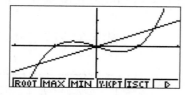

Figure 3.22 G-Solve

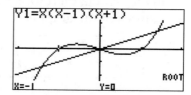

Figure 3.23 Root

Press [[F5]:G-Solve] for the soft menu choices to return to the screen. [[F2]:MAX] places the cursor on the maximum value of the function and [[F3]:MIN] places it on the minimum value of the function. [[F3]:Y-ICPT] moves the cursor to the function's y-intercept.

   Press [[F5]:ISCT]. The cursor automatically advances to the first point of intersection of the two graphs and the equations of the two graphs being used are once again displayed at the top of the screen. To move to the next intersection point, the **right replay arrow** must be pressed. Continue to press the **replay arrows** to see the value of each intersection. Press [[F5]:G-Solv] to return to the G-Solve menu screen.

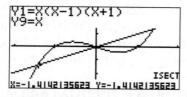

Figure 3.24 First Intersection Point

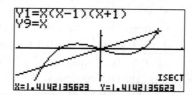

Figure 3.25 Third Intersection Point

   Press [[F6]: ▶] followed by [[F1]:Y-CAL] [EXE]. The equation of the function being used is displayed at the top before pressing [EXE] and "$x = $" is displayed on the lower left corner of the screen after pressing [EXE]. Enter any value for x, say 3, and press [EXE]. The displayed words, "Not Found," mean that the value of x chosen is not on the viewing screen. Return to the soft menu screen by pressing [[F5]:G-Solv] [[F6]: ▶]

[F1 :Y-CAL] EXE . Now enter 1.5 for *x*. The answer of 1.875 is displayed. [[F2 :X-CAL] evaluates the value for *x* when *y* is the input.

- **G↔T**

[F6]:[G↔T] allows the user to toggle between the text (graph stack) and the graph screen.

3.3.4 Using Color to Distinguish Graphs

The greatest integer function and the function obtained by using the integer part of the number cannot be easily separated if both are drawn on the same screen in the same color. Select Y7 and Y8 and unselect Y1 and Y9. In the section on changing a graph's color, Y7 was given the color of green and Y8 was given the color of orange. Since both Y7 and Y8 are piecewise functions, change the Graph Set Up to Plot. To do this press SHIFT [MENU:SETUP] while in the *Graph Menu.* With **Draw Type** highlighted, press [F2 :PLOT] EXIT . Change the V-Window to [F3 :STD] and draw the graphs.

Now select Y2 and r3, unselect Y7 and Y8, change the V-Window to [F2 :TRIG], and the **Graph Set Up** back to connected. Y2 should be drawn in blue and r3 in orange. Draw the graphs. Now draw the same graph by pressing [F2 :ZOOM] [F6 : ▶] [F2 :SQR]. It can be seen in both cases that color allows the two graphs to be visually separated from one another on the screen, but different view screens also allow for a better graph.

3.3.5 Using the Dual Screen with Graphs

The Sketch command accessed by the soft menu key F4 is one way to sketch the inverse of a relation. Another way is to use parametric equations. Unselect all functions previously sketched. Replace the function in Y1 with $y = x^2$. To do this, activate the graph stack and highlight Y1. Press X,θ,T x^2 EXE . The new function will replace the previous one. Draw this function on [F1 :INIT] under the V-Window menu.

Press SHIFT [MENU:SETUP]. Highlight Dual Screen on the Set Up menu. Press [F1 :Grph]. The dual screen has been activated to be used with graphs. Another choice is to use a table with the graph. Press EXIT and [F6 :DRAW]. Press OPTN to see the options available. When graphing, the left screen is active while the right screen is passive. At any time the viewing scale can be changed by selecting SHIFT [F3 :V-Window] and selecting either right or left.

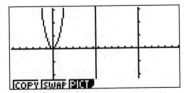

Figure 3.26 Dual Graph

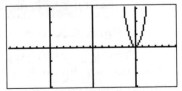

Figure 3.27 Dual Swap

Press [F2 :SWAP] to move the drawn function to the passive screen. Press EXIT to return to the graph stack and select the parametric equation in position 4. Press SHIFT [F3 :V-Window] and press [F3 :STD]. Press EXIT [F6 :DRAW]. Note that only a part of graph 4 was drawn. To correct this, return to [F3 :V-Window]. The range data is given for the left screen. Arrow down to the second screen of the range.

Observe that 'T' is starting at zero which does not allow for negative values. Enter the number −5 for the min of T and 5 for the max of T, then return to draw by pressing EXIT [F6 :DRAW].

Figure 3.28 Inverse Relation

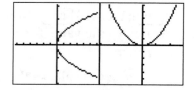

Figure 3.29 Adjusted V-Window

To get the left side to look more like the inverse relation of the right side, switch the *x* and *y* min and *x* and *y* max on the left side V-Window.

Try using one of the zoom commands while in split window. The original function will stay on the left and the zoomed part of the function will appear on the right. All functions available to the calculator are also available on the active side of the screen. The G↔T key, however, in split screen acts as a 3-way toggle. It will enlarge the left side to full screen, the right side to full screen and will return the screen to the graph stack.

Before leaving this section, return to SET UP and turn off Dual Screen.

3.3.6   Exploring the Dynamic Graphing Mode

Return to the menu by pressing [EXIT] until the calculator no longer responds, then press [MENU]. Activate menu number 6, *Dyna Menu.* This is the menu known as the dynamic graphing menu. Observe that all the graphs entered on the graph stack are available in this menu. Unselect any graphs that may have been selected. Arrow to function line Y10. If the type is not rectangular, make this change. Enter Y10 = $A(x + B)^2 + C$ using the alpha keys to enter *A, B,* and *C* and using the [X,θ,T] key for *x*. Press [EXE] to put this equation on the stack. Set the viewing window to STD.

The purpose of the dynamic grapher is to observe the change a function makes when the value of a variable changes. Press [[F4]:VAR] and select the variable *B* by highlighting the *B* and pressing [[F1]:SEL]. By selecting *B* the horizontal movement of the graph will be observed. Enter constant values for *A* and *C* on this screen. Let *A* = 1 and *C* = 2. Enter one number followed by the execute key then arrow down to the next value to be entered. Enter the number and press [EXE]. [Note: It is not necessary to enter a value for the variable which is varying.]

Figure 3.30 Dynamic Equation

Figure 3.31 Dynamic Variable

Press [[F2]:RANG] to set the range of movement. Enter −5 for the start and 5 for the end. Set the pitch at 1. (This means that the graph will move from −5 to 5 every integer unit.) [EXIT] and press [[F3]:SPEED]. Stop and Go allows the user to look at the position and press the execute key to move the graph to each new position. Select normal speed by highlighting normal and pressing [EXE].

Finally, press [[F6]:DYNA] to see the movement of the graph. The calculator displays a "time line" while it is preparing the graph.

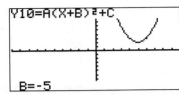

Figure 3.32 Position when $B = -5$

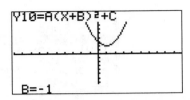

Figure 3.33 Position when $B = -1$

To stop the graph, press [AC/ON]. This command will return the view screen to a menu where the start and end values can be changed. To return to the original screen, press [EXIT]. Be careful, however, the variable to be changed has reverted back to A and must be selected again.

3.4   Tables and Lists

In the previous section on exploring graphs, the split screen feature was introduced to be used with graphs. In this section the use of the split screen with tables will be explored.

3.4.1   Creating Tables

Tables may be created by using **Table Menu** or created from the pixels on a graph while in the **Dual Screen** feature of the **Graph Menu.**

- **Using the Table Menu**

Return the calculator's screen to show the **Main Menu.** Activate menu item number 7, **Table Menu.** The graph stack is once again displayed with all equations present from previous use. This allows the user to work in several modes and do many operations with the same functions. Since the graph stack is getting cluttered with previous operations, delete all functions. This will allow this section to be presented with a "clean slate."

Enter the following rectangular functions on the stack:

$$Y1 = x(x + 1)(x - 1) \qquad Y2 = x^2 - 3x + 4 \qquad Y3 = x$$

Press [[F5]:RANG] to set the parameters of the table. Enter the starting value of x at -5 and the ending value at 5. The pitch indicates how often a value in the table is needed; change this value to 0.5. Press [EXIT] to return to the soft menu screen and [[F6]:TABL] to obtain a table of values for each of the selected functions.

Arrow up and down the x-values of the functions and compare the three. Are there any values where all y-values are the same? Are there any values where one of the functions becomes zero? Where do the values change from positive to negative? Observe that Y2 does not appear to cross the x-axis. (The function values are always positive.) Are there any other significant similarities or differences among the three functions?

Tables allow a visual study of a function without sketching its graph. However, if the graph of the function is also required, simply press either [[F5]:G-CON] or [[F6]:G-PLT] for graph connected or graph plot, respectively.

- **Using the Dual Screen**

Return to **Graph Menu** and press [SHIFT][[MENU]:SET UP]. Highlight **Dual Screen** and press [[F2]:G to T]. This activates the Dual Screen Mode to be used to create tables from graphs.

[EXIT] and press [[F6]:DRAW]. Press [[F1]:Trace]. Arrow until a desired x-value is reached. Press [EXE]. This will record the y-value for every function on the screen to the table even though only Y1 is visible on the Dual Screen table.

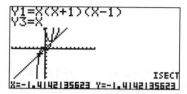

Figure 3.34 G to T Dual Screen

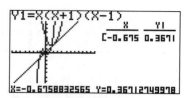

Figure 3.35 Graph to Table

The G-Solve features can be used in Dual Screen; therefore an intersection can be found and recorded in the table by pressing [EXE]. The first intersection point of Y1 and Y3 is shown in Figure 3.36. To see the table of values for all three functions, press [OPTN] [[F1]:CHG] [[F6]:G↔T] [[F6]:G↔T].

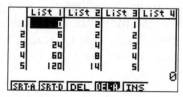

Figure 3.36 Intersection Point

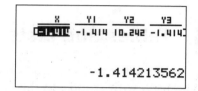

Figure 3.37 Table of All Functions

3.4.2 Creating Lists

To create a list, return to the **Main Menu** and activate menu item number 4, **List Menu**. Lists may be created in several ways. For example, a list may be created from a stored function, from a sequence, or by simply entering the data. There are 6 columns in which to enter lists. Before a list may be stored from another function of the calculator, the List column must be empty. Delete any lists previously in the calculator by pressing [[F4]:DEL-A] [[F1]:YES].

To enter a list from a stored function, press [MENU] and the number 7 to enter the **Table Menu.** The three functions previously used should still be on the stack. Press [[F6]:TABL] to activate the table generated by the functions. Restructure the table for integer values of x from 1 to 10 by pressing [EXIT][[F5]:RANG]. Change the start value to 1, end value to 10, and pitch to 1. Press [EXIT][[F6]:TABL]. The table is now in integer increments from 1 to 10. Highlight any number under Y1 and press [OPTN]. Press [[F1]:LIST] [[F2]:LMEM] [[F1]:List1]. The function values for Y1 are now stored in List 1. Repeat the procedure for Y2 and Y3 to store them in List 2 and List 3, respectively. That is, highlight a value under Y2, press [[F2]:LMEM] [[F2]:List2]; highlight a value under Y3, press [[F2]:LMEM] [[F3]:List3]. To verify that the functions are stored in the required lists, return to the **Main Menu** and activate the **List Menu.** See figure 3.38.

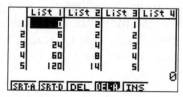

Figure 3.38 Stored Lists

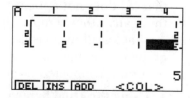

Figure 3.39 Operations with Lists

Lists can also be created from sequence functions. Return to the **Main Menu** and activate the **Recursion Menu** (number 8). To store the arithmetic sequence with $a_1 = 2$ and a common difference of 3 in List 4, press [[F3]:TYPE] [[F1]:a_n] and enter 2 [+] 3 [( ] [[F4]:n] [—] 1 [ )] [EXE]. Press [[F5]:RANG] and set the start at 1 and the end at 10. Press [EXE][[F6]:TABL]. To store the result in List 4, press [OPTN] [[F1]:LIST]. Highlight a number under a_n and press [[F2]:LMEM] [[F4]:List4].

Experiment by putting other sequences into Lists and by just entering the elements of a desired list. Then return to the ***Run Menu*** and work with the lists as described in section 1 of this chapter.

3.5 Equations and Systems of Equations

Equations were solved when the soft menu keys were introduced under the ***Graph Menu.*** For example, the function $y = x(x + 1)(x - 1)$ was entered on the graph stack and its roots were found using [[F5]:G-Solv]. The equation was further studied using the trace function and zoom features.

3.5.1 Using the Equation Menu

The equation $y = x(x + 1)(x - 1)$ can also be solved by using the ***Equa Menu.*** Activate this menu by highlighting menu A on the ***Main Menu*** screen and pressing [EXE]. Press [[F2]:POLY] for the polynomial choice, followed by [F2] for a third degree equation. The equation needs to be rewritten as $y = x^3 - x$ in order to enter the coefficients into the data form. On the data matrix enter 1 [EXE] 0 [EXE] [(−)] 1 [EXE] 0 [EXE]. Press [[F1]:SOLV]. The answer immediately appears on the screen.

To solve a system of equations using this menu, [EXIT] until the choice screen is reached. This time press [[F1]:SIML]. Press [F2] to indicate that there will be three equations. The following system will be used to demonstrate this menu.

$$\begin{cases} x + y + 2z = 1 \\ x + y + z = 2 \\ 2x - y + z = 5 \end{cases}$$

Enter the coefficients and constants of the first equation across the top, the values for the second equation in the second row, and finally, the values for the third equation in the third row. Thus, enter 1 [EXE] 1 [EXE] 2 [EXE] 1 [EXE]; 1 [EXE] 1 [EXE] 1 [EXE] 2 [EXE]; 2 [EXE] [(−)] 1 [EXE] 1 [EXE] 5 [EXE]. Press [[F1]:SOLV] to see the result of (3,0,−1). [EXIT] three times and press [MENU].

3.5.2 Using Matrices to Solve Systems

- **Using the Inverse of a Matrix**

Systems of two equations in two unknowns can be solved using G-Solv and [ISECT]. However, the three equation system previously solved cannot be solved on this calculator by graphs. With the ***Main Menu*** on the screen, activate the ***Mat Menu*** (item number 3).

A list of matrix locations appears. With location A highlighted type 3 [EXE] 3 [EXE] to enter a dimension of 3 × 3 for matrix A. Enter the coefficients of the variables as in the previous example, without entering the constants. That is, 1 [EXE] 1 [EXE] 2 [EXE]; 1 [EXE] 1 [EXE] 1 [EXE]; 2 [EXE] [(−)] 1 [EXE] 1 [EXE]. [EXIT] to return to the matrix list. Highlight location B and type 3 [EXE] 1 [EXE], then enter the constants in the column matrix displayed. 1 [EXE] 2 [EXE] 5 [EXE].

Activate the ***Run Menu*** and press [OPTN] [[F2]:MAT] [[F1]:Mat] [ALPHA] [[X,θ,T]:A] [SHIFT] [[ )]:x^{-1}] [EXE]. This result is the inverse of matrix A. Store this matrix in location C by pressing [[F1]:Mat] [SHIFT] [[(−)]:ANS] [→] [[F1]:Mat] [ALPHA] [ln:C] [EXE].

To find the solution, simply multiply the inverse of A (Matrix C) times the Constant Matrix (Matrix B). That is, press [[F1]:Mat] [ALPHA] [ln:C] [×] [[F1]:Mat] [ALPHA] [[LOG]:B] [EXE]. The same result of (3,0,−1) is displayed.

- ## Using Elementary Row Operations

Activate the **Matrix Menu.** Display the matrix stored in location A by pressing [EXE] when it is highlighted. Highlight any number in column 3 and press [[F3]:COL] [[F3]:ADD]. This will add a 4th column to the columns of matrix A. Enter the constants of the system in this new column. Matrix A should now look like the matrix displayed in Figure 3.40.

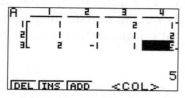

Figure 3.40 Matrix Entries

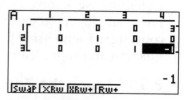

Figure 3.41 Matrix Row Operations

Press [EXIT] [[F1]:R-OP] to activate the row operations commands. Press [[F3]:XR w +]. This command multiplies a row by a real number and adds the result to another row. The object is to get 1's in the a_{ii} positions and 0's for all other entries in the coefficient matrix. Enter [(−)] 1 [EXE] 1 [EXE] 2 [EXE]. (That is, multiply row 1 times −1 and add it to row 2.) The result is immediate. Press [F3] again and enter [(−)] 2 [EXE] 1 [EXE] 3 [EXE]. (Multiply row 1 times −2 and add the result to row 3.) Press [[F1]:Swap]. Press 2 [EXE] 3 [EXE] to swap rows 2 and 3. Press [[F2]:XRow]. Enter [(−)] 1 [a%] 3 [EXE] 2 [EXE] to multiply row 2 by −1/3. Press [[F3]:XR w +]. Enter [(−)] 1 [EXE] 2 [EXE] 1 [EXE].

Moving to the third column, press [[F4]:R w +]. Enter 3 [EXE] 1 [EXE]. (This adds row three to row 1.) Press [F4] again and enter 3 [EXE] 2 [EXE]. Finally press [F2] one more time and enter [(−)] 1 [EXE] 3 [EXE]. The same answer is present once again this time in column four of the matrix. See figure 3.41.

CHAPTER

4

Graphing with the HP 48G

This chapter introduces the graphing and solving capabilities of the HP 48G and HP 48GX graphing-symbolic calculators. The two models differ primarily in that the HP 48GX has more random access memory (RAM) (128K RAM vs. 32K RAM for the 48G) and has two expansion ports for additional RAM or read-only memory (ROM). In this chapter, both calculators are referred to as the HP 48G.

Like its predecessors, the HP 48S and HP 48SX, the HP 48G is a sophisticated, general purpose, mathematics calculator. Unlike its predecessors, however, the HP 48G does not require a much larger learning-time investment than other calculators on the market. This is because of its extensive use of pull-down menus and options and on-screen prompts.

Before reading the rest of this chapter, you are encouraged to read Chapters 1–3 in the *HP 48G Series User's Guide* that came with your calculator. These chapters will give you a working knowledge of stack operations and variables. If you are not familiar with reverse polish notation, then you are especially encouraged to refer to Chapter 3 in the User's Manual. The flexibility of the HP 48G and its encyclopedic capabilities make it difficult to give the reader a complete picture of its possible applications.

4.1 HP 48G Fundamentals

4.1.1 Using the Multipurpose [ON] Key

Press [ON] to turn on your calculator. This key not only turns the HP 48G on but also acts as a **general purpose interruption key** (note the word CANCEL written below the key). It halts calculator execution and returns to a previous state. For example, when you are entering a number, pressing [ON] clears the number and returns to the previous stack display.

Any time the calculator is in a state you want to abandon, press [ON] one or more times, and it will eventually return to its default state, showing the stack. If the calculator beeps and shows an error message, press [ON] to remove the message.

Press [→] [OFF] to turn off the calculator. The [OFF] key is a **shifted** (the green [→] key) version of the [ON] key.

4.1.2 Adjusting the Display contrast

With the calculator on, hold down [ON] and press [+] to darken or [−] to lighten the display.

4.1.3 Exploring the HP 48G Keyboard

Most of the 49 keys on the HP 48G performs more than one function. A key's primary function is printed in white on the key itself. Simply pressing a key activates this function. A key's other functions are printed above the key in green and/or purple. To access these functions, press the purple ⟨⇐⟩ or the green ⟨⇒⟩ before pressing the key. For example, press

⟨⇒⟩ [PLOT]

to activate the PLOT application. Finally, a key's alphabetic function, if any, is printed in white below and to the right of the key and is accessed using ⟨α⟩ (Alpha-Shift). For example, to type an uppercase X on the screen press

⟨α⟩ ⟨1/x⟩.

A lowercase letter can be accessed by pressing ⟨α⟩ ⟨⇐⟩ before entering the letter.

The exceptions to these rules are the menu keys, which are the blank, white keys in the top row of the keyboard. Although these keys do have fixed alphabetic functions (A–F), their other functions vary from application to application. For example, pressing ⟨MTH⟩ displays the first six labels shown in (Fig. 4.1), while the second set of labels is made visible via ⟨NXT⟩ (see Fig. 4.2).

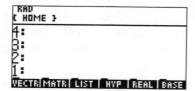

Figure 4.1

Figure 4.2

Notice that each of these labels has a small tab at the top left corner. This signifies they are file folders that contain other options and/or other file folders. To continue our current example, return to the first six MTH labels and press [B: MATR] to activate the MATR folder which contains folders and options for matrices, as shown here in Fig. 4.3.

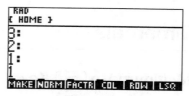

Figure 4.3

These new folders contain options such as the LSQ option as well as other file folders such as the COL folder that contains even more options (→COL, COL→, COL+, etc). Finally, note that on the keyboard the major applications, such as PLOT and SOLVE, are all grouped together and associated with the numerical keys 1–9.

4.2 Learning the Graphing Essentials

Since the HP 48G makes extensive use of pull-down menus and on-screen prompts, many of its operational procedures are self-explanatory. Therefore this section is devoted mainly to examples that illustrate the HP 48G's wide range of graphing capabilities.

4.2.1 The Plot Application

To demonstrate this application we will start with a simple example: graphing the function

$$Y = \sin(X).$$

Press

$$\boxed{\rightarrow} \; [\text{PLOT}]$$

to activate the PLOT menu as shown in Fig. 4.4.

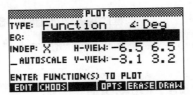

Figure 4.4

Notice the on-screen prompt that reads 'ENTER FUNCTION(S) TO PLOT' as well as the highlight bar positioned to the right of 'EQ:'. *EQ* is a reserved variable that contains a list of the functions to be plotted. Also notice the option labels at the bottom of the screen. The EDIT option, [A:EDIT] allows you to edit the current (in this case, empty) expression; the CHOOS option, [B:CHOOS] allows you to choose an expression or list from among those that are currently saved in user memory. In our next example, we demonstrate how to save an expression more permanently in user memory; in this example, we will simply save our expression temporarily in the variable *EQ*. Press [A:EDIT] to place an insert cursor between two tick marks on the screen's command line (see Fig. 4.5). The tick marks, ' ', are used to begin and end any algebraic object. To enter our expression, press

$$\boxed{\text{SIN}} \; \boxed{\alpha} \; [\text{X}]$$

(see Fig. 4.6) and then press $\boxed{\text{ENTER}}$. The highlight bar then moves to the next option, the independent variable (INDEP), and the on-screen prompt changes to 'ENTER INDEPENDENT VAR [iable] NAME' (see Fig. 4.7).

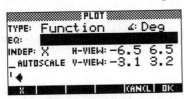

Figure 4.5

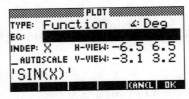

Figure 4.6

Figure 4.7

The cursor-movement keys move the highlight bar to any option on the PLOT menu. For example, to change the angle units from degrees to radians, press

$$\boxed{\blacktriangleleft} \; \boxed{\blacktriangleleft} \; [\text{B:CHOOS}] \; \boxed{\blacktriangledown} \; \boxed{\text{ENTER}}.$$

See Figs. 4.8–4.10.

Figure 4.8

Figure 4.9

Figure 4.10

Press [E:ERASE] and [F:DRAW] to see the plot (Fig. 4.11).

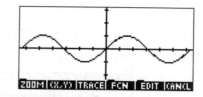
Figure 4.11

4.2.2 The Interactive Plot Mode

Once a graph is plotted, the calculator does not return to the stack; instead it enters what is called the Interactive Plot mode, which allows the user to explore and add graphical elements to the plot. While in this mode, the keyboard is redefined for graphical purposes, as follows:

1. The cursor-movement keys [◄] [▲] [▼] [►] move the cursor in the indicated direction. Preceding a cursor key with [→] moves the cursor to the edge of the screen in the indicated direction.

2. [−] removes the folder/option labels so that all of the graph screen is visible. This is a toggle key, so pressing it again will retrieve the labels.

3. [+] displays the cursor coordinates. It also is a toggle key.

4. [←] [CLEAR] erases the plotted graph from the screen, it does not, however, erase the cursor, which remains active. To recover the graph, press

    [ON] [F:DRAW].

5. [ENTER] places the cursor coordinates on the stack.

4.2.3 Tracing

As you can see from the labels, the HP 48G has a TRACE feature. To activate this feature, press

    [C:TRACE].

Notice that a small highlighted square appears on the TRACE folder label (see Fig. 4.12). Press

    [B:(X,Y)]

and use [◄] and [►] to move the cursor along the curve (see Fig. 4.13). To retrieve the labels, press any menu key. To deactivate the TRACE feature, press [C:TRACE] again. Note that the highlighted square disappears as shown in Fig. 4.14.

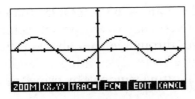

Figure 4.12

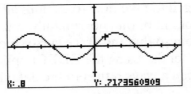

Figure 4.13

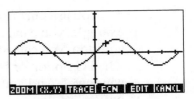

Figure 4.14

4.2.4 Zooming

To continue our example, press

[A:ZOOM]

to access the extensive zoom capabilities of the HP 48G. To change both the horizontal and vertical zoom factors to 5 press

[A:ZFACT] 5 [ENTER] 5 [ENTER] [C:CHK]

(see Fig. 4.15). Press

[F:OK] [C:ZIN]

to zoom-in by a factor of 5, as shown in Fig. 4.16.

Figure 4.15

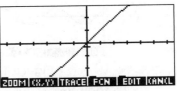

Figure 4.16

Before proceeding, zoom-out again to the default settings by pressing

[A:ZOOM] [D:ZOUT].

One option in the ZOOM folder is the ZTrig option. Press

[A:ZOOM] [NXT] [NXT] [C:ZTRIG]

(see Fig. 4.17).
With our original expression and the default plot parameters, the ZTrig option sets the horizontal step to $\pi/20$. Press

[C:TRACE] [B:(X,Y)]

and press [▶] ten times to display the value of SIN(X) when $x = \pi/2$ (see Fig. 4.18).

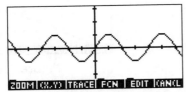

Figure 4.17

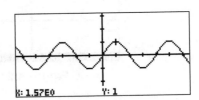

Figure 4.18

You are encouraged to take time to explore all the options in the ZOOM folder. For example, you can zoom-in or out, horizontally and/or vertically to any preset factor. In addition, you can zoom so that the Trace cursor moves through integer abscissas using the ZINTG option or by tenths, using the ZDECI option, effectively creating "friendly windows." And you can always return to the default plotting windows by using the ZDFLT option.

Two of the most useful options are the ZSQR option, which changes the range so that the scale on each axis is the same, and the BOXZ option, which allows the user to pick a rectangular area that then becomes the viewing window. To return to our example, press any menu key to retrieve the labels, then press

$$[A:ZOOM] \ [E:ZSQR]$$

(see Fig. 4.19). Press

$$[B:(X,Y)] \ \boxed{\blacktriangleright}$$

to move the cursor along the *x*-axis until you reach $x = \pi/2 \approx 1.57$. Next press $\boxed{\blacktriangle}$ to move the cursor up until it lies directly across from the first tick mark on the *y*-axis. Doing this enables you to see that the cursor, the first tick marks on each axis, and the origin are indeed the vertices of a square (see Fig. 4.20).

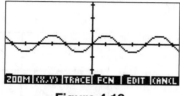

Figure 4.19

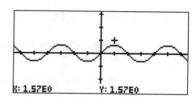

Figure 4.20

To zoom in on this square, press any menu key to retrieve the labels, then press

$$[A: ZOOM] \ [B:BOXZ].$$

The point $(\pi/2, \pi/2)$ has already been established as one corner of the viewing window. Move the cursor down to the *x*-axis. Notice that a vertical segment follows the cursor. Next, move the cursor left towards the origin (see Fig. 4.21). Notice the zoom box is beginning to form. Continue moving the cursor until it is positioned at the origin, then press

$$[F:ZOOM]$$

to obtain the display shown in Fig. 4.22. Notice that the square has been stretched horizontally to fit the rectangular viewing window.

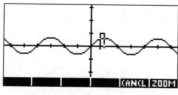

Figure 4.21

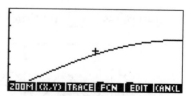

Figure 4.22

4.3 Additional Graphing Capabilities

The following sections, although not an exhaustive accounting of all of the HP 48G's graphing capabilities, will give you a working familiarity with some of the many features. Before continuing, press

[ON] [▼] [▼] [▶] [DEL] [▼] [F:OK]

to reset the plot window to its default settings.

4.3.1 Using the Catalog

As mentioned before, you can store an expression, equation, or list in the reserved variable *EQ* on a temporary basis only. If the expression in *EQ* is changed, the old expression is overwritten and lost to the user. Often, it is useful to look at the plots of several functions at once or to store one or more functions more permanently. Suppose you want to look at the plots of both $x \cdot \sin(x)$ and $\cos(x)$. Use the cursor-movement keys to move the highlight bar to the current equation (*EQ*). Press

[B:CHOOS]

to see a display like that shown in Fig. 4.23. You may have other objects in memory, so your display may not match the one pictured exactly.

Figure 4.23

Press

[D:NEW]

(see Fig. 4.24). To enter the first expression 'X∗SIN(X)', press

['] [α] [X] [×] [SIN] [α] [X] [ENTER]

Figure 4.24

and give it the name 'F' by pressing

[α] [F] [ENTER]

(see Fig. 4.25). Press [F:OK] to place this new function at the top of the catalog (see Fig. 4.26).

Figure 4.25

Figure 4.26

Follow the same process to place 'COS(X)' in the catalog under the name 'G'. Press

[D:NEW] ['] cos α [X] ENTER α [G] ENTER [F:OK]

(see Fig. 4.27).

Figure 4.27

To plot both of these functions, press

[C:√CHK]

to place a check mark next to the function 'G'; then press

▼ [C:√CHK]

to move the highlight bar down to 'F' and check it (see Fig. 4.28). Press

[F:OK]

to accept your choices. Note that *EQ* is now a list containing the two functions *F* and *G*. Also, note that our original expression, 'SIN(X)', which had been in *EQ*, has been dropped. It is no longer in memory (see Fig. 4.29). On the other hand, if we were to place another function in *EQ*, *F* and *G* would still be in the catalog list, accessed by the CHOOS option. Press [E:ERASE] [F:DRAW] to see the plots (see Fig.4.30).

Figure 4.28 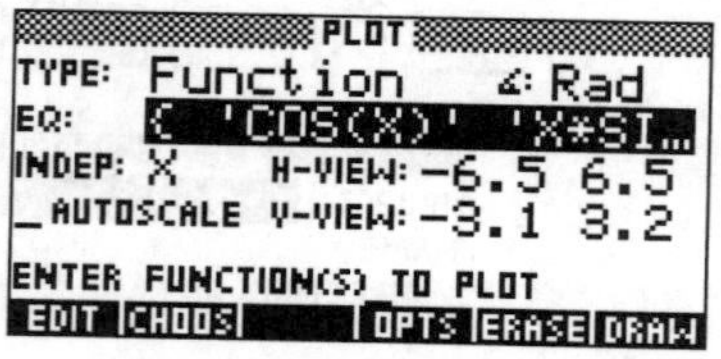 **Figure 4.29** 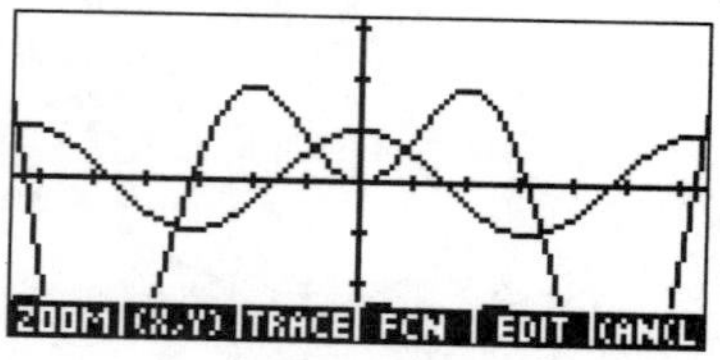 **Figure 4.30**

In this example, the plots were drawn sequentially. To draw the plots simultaneously, press

ON [D:OPTS]

to reach the PLOT OPTIONS menu. Move the highlight bar to 'SIMULT' and press [C:√CHK] to activate this option (see Fig. 4.31), followed by [F:OK] to return to the main PLOT menu. Then press [E:ERASE] [F:DRAW] to redraw the plots simultaneously.

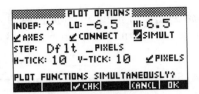

Figure 4.31

4.3.2 The Function Folder

To continue our example, press

[D:FCN]

to see the options available in the FCN (functions) folder (see Fig. 4.32). Press NXT to see the rest of the options (see Fig. 4.33). Most of the options in this folder are concerned with characteristics of the graphs of functions.

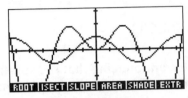

Figure 4.32

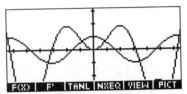

Figure 4.33

Because the first function in the list presently in EQ is $\cos(x)$, pressing

NXT [A:ROOT]

will find a root of $y = \cos(x)$ that lies nearest to the cursor, which is now at its default location at $(0, 0)$. The cursor moves to the root, and the bottom line of the screen flashes the message 'SIGN REVERSAL' to indicate that the solution was estimated within the limits of the machine. The bottom line then displays the root value 1.57079632679, which is approximately equal to $\pi/2$ (see Fig. 4.34). Press any menu key to restore the option labels.

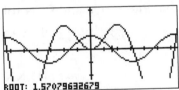

Figure 4.34

You can switch to the other function 'X∗SIN(X)', by pressing NXT to retrieve the rest of the FCN options as shown in Fig. 4.35, then press

[D:NXEQ].

The bottom line of the screen now displays the expression 'X∗SIN(X)' and the cursor jumps vertically to the plot of the new function (see Fig. 4.36). Press any menu key to restore the labels.

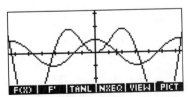

Figure 4.35

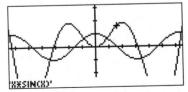

Figure 4.36

To find the root of $x \cdot \sin(x)$ near $x = 3$. Press $\boxed{+}$ $\boxed{+}$ to set the coordinates, then move the cursor near $x = 3$, and press any menu key followed by

$$\boxed{\text{NXT}} \text{ [A:ROOT]},$$

and see 'ROOT':3.14159265359', which is approximately equal to π (see Fig. 4.37).

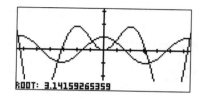

Figure 4.37

Again, press any menu key to restore the labels.

To locate the nearest intersection of the two plots at (3.42561845948, -.9599350991) press

$$\boxed{+} \text{ [B:ISECT]}$$

(see Fig. 4.38).

Again, the sign reversal message flashes briefly, announcing that the solution is an approximation. The values of the roots and the intersections of the plots are all placed on the stack automatically. Press $\boxed{\text{ON}}$ repeatedly until you return to the stack (see Fig. 4.39, your menu label may differ).

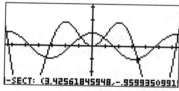

Figure 4.38

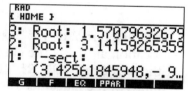

Figure 4.39

Return to the Interactive Plot mode and FCN folder by pressing

$$\boxed{\rightarrow} \boxed{\text{PLOT}} \text{ [F:DRAW] [D:FCN]}.$$

Then press

$$\boxed{\text{NXT}} \text{ [D:NXEQ]}$$

to return to the cosine function, and then press any menu key to retrieve the menu labels. Press $\boxed{\text{NXT}}$ [F:EXTR] to find the nearest maximum or minimum of the current function, in our case the maximum of 1 for $\cos(x)$ at $x = 0$ (see Fig.4.40).

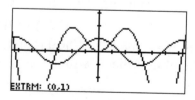

Figure 4.40

4.4 Polar Graphing

Thanks to the pull-down menus, polar graphing on the HP 48G is easier than it was on the HP 48S. Press [ON] to return to the PLOT application, then press [▲] to move the highlight bar to the equation 'TYPE' and press [B:CHOOS] to see the list of options. Use the cursor-movement keys to highlight 'Polar' and press [ENTER].

EXAMPLE 1

Problem Graph the limacon $r = 1.5(1 - 2\cos\theta)$.

Solution Move the highlight bar to the current equation, by pressing [▼]. Press

$$[\,'\,]\ [\alpha]\ [Y]\ [\Leftarrow][=]\ 1\ [\cdot]\ 5\ [\times]\ [\Leftarrow][(\,)]\ 1\ [-]\ 2\ [\times]\ [\cos]$$
$$[\alpha]\ [X]\ [\text{ENTER}]$$

to obtain 'Y = 1.5*(1 − 2*COS(X))' as the equation *EQ*. Because the default interval for θ is $[0, 2\pi]$, press

$$[\text{E:ERASE}]\ [\text{F:DRAW}]$$

to see the plot. Press [−] to remove the labels (see Fig. 4.41).

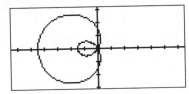

Figure 4.41

4.5 Parametric Graphing

As with polar graphing, pull-down menus have simplified the plotting of parametric graphs.

EXAMPLE 2

Problem Graph the Lissajous figure $x = 3\sin(3t)$, $y = 2\sin(4t)$ for $0 \le t \le 6.5$.

Solution Press [ON] to leave the Interactive Plot mode and return to the PLOT application, then use the cursor-movement keys to move the highlight bar to 'TYPE'. Press

$$[\text{B:CHOOS}],$$

use the cursor-movement keys to move the highlight bar to 'Parametric' and press [ENTER] (see Fig. 4.42).

Figure 4.42

The equation must be entered in the form $(x(t), y(t))$. Move the highlight bar to 'EQ' and press

['] [←] [()] 3 [×] [SIN] 3 [×] [α] [←] [T] [▶] [←] [,]
2 [×] [SIN] 4 [×] [α] [←] [T] [ENTER]

to obtain

'(3*SIN(3*t), 2*SIN(4*t))'.

Your screen will not show the entire expression. Change the independent variable to 't' by moving the highlight bar to 'INDEP' and pressing

[α] [←] [T] [F:OK].

Press

[E:ERASE] [F:DRAW]

to see the plot (see Fig. 4.43).

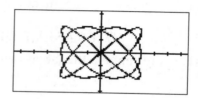

Figure 4.43

4.6 Conclusion

The foregoing sections have described only a fraction of the capabilities of the HP 48G. In addition to the catalog of user-defined functions, there is an Equation Library in ROM that is accessed by pressing [→] [EQ LIB] from the home screen. Equations in this library are grouped by topic name. When it is advantageous, the equations have accompanying diagrams to identify the variables. There also is an extensive UNITS application, where values can be tagged with units. The HP 48G then keeps track of the units and changes them appropriately as calculations are made. An extensive STAT (statistical) application is also available, as well as a SYMBOLIC application, which allows the user to do everything from symbolic differentiation to symbolic manipulation of an algebraic expression. Finally, the HP 48G can print graphs, etc., to a thermal printer via the infrared Input/Output port (like using your TV remote control). The I/O port also can be used to transfer programs and any other information (like matrices) from one HP 48 to another. Cables also are available that will allow you to transfer files to and from either a PC-compatible or a Macintosh computer. The owner's manual contains information on all of these topics.

C H A P T E R

5

The HP 38G Graphing Calculator

The Hewlett-Packard HP 38G is a flexible tool for exploring mathematical topics from algebra through calculus. Algebraic entry and total recall of previous computations make this machine easy to use, while built-in applications for everything from graphing to table-building make the HP 38G a complete mathematical tool. This chapter will introduce you to the basic structure and functionality of the calculator. Have your calculator handy as you read through the following pages. It is not necessary to read the sections in order; feel free to browse.

5.1   Getting Started with the HP 38G

5.1.1   The Keyboard

The HP 38G keyboard basically contains nine rows of keys with up to six keys in each row. The top row of keys are blank. These are called menu label keys because their function changes as you change menus on the display. The first three keys in the second row reflect an emphasis on exploring mathematics graphically [PLOT], symbolically or algebraically [SYMB], and numerically [NUM]. The first three keys in the third row open the doors to the calculator's advanced capabilities. The next six rows contain the traditional functionality found on scientific calculators. Under the [ENTER] key, there is a column of keys that require some mention. This column contains the alpha-shift and blue-shift keys. The alpha shift, A...Z, allows you to make alphabetical entries, while the blue shift allows you to access the commands or menus printed in blue above the various keys. Below these are the [DEL] key for deleting characters and the [ON] key. Notice that the blue shift of the [DEL] key is [CLEAR], for cleaning up entire screens at once instead of just deleting one character in the command line or one field in a menu. Also notice that the blue shift of the [ON] key will turn the calculator off. Of course, the calculator will also shut itself off after a few minutes if no keys are pressed.

5.1.2   Display Basics

This [ON] key turns the calculator on, but it has other purposes as well. Pressing the [ON] key while typing in the command line will clear what has been typed. Holding down the [ON] key while pressing the [−] or [+] keys will decrease or increase the contrast of the display, respectively. Finally, the [HOME] key will take you back to the computational screen.

5.2 Computations and Editing

5.2.1 The Home Screen

The home screen is divided into four areas. At the top is the annunciator bar, with the home screen title as well as an annunciator that tells you whether angle measures are in degrees or radians. Below this is the computational window, where your computations are displayed. A line at the bottom of the computations window separates it from the command line, wherein all computations are originally entered. Finally, at the very bottom of the screen, there is a row of up to six menu labels. These labels tell you what the functions, if any, the top row of blank keys will perform at any given moment.

5.2.2 Working in the Home Screen

The HP 38G is a straightforward, algebraic entry calculator. In most cases, you just enter expressions as you see them in your text. For instance, to calculate $3 + 4\sin(20°)$, simply press 3 $\boxed{+}$ 4 $\boxed{\text{SIN}}$ 20 $\boxed{\text{ENTER}}$. Of course, you must be in degree mode (see page 83). It is not necessary to enter the multiplication symbol. In most cases, juxtaposition implies multiplication. Also, it is not necessary to supply the final right parenthesis. While the expression is being entered in the command line, it contains a blank where the multiplication should be (Figure 5.1). After the $\boxed{\text{ENTER}}$ key is pressed, the expression is changed so that it not only contains that multiplication symbol explicitly, but also has the final right parenthesis (Figure 5.2).

Figure 5.1

Figure 5.2

The numerical approximation, 4.368 . . . , is displayed below the expression. The first label in the menu at the bottom of the display is now STO▶, in case you wish to save this result in a variable. Suppose that you wish to edit the original expression so that it reads $3 + 4\sin(35°)$ instead. It is not necessary to type in the entire expression. All computations are available to you at any time. Simply use the up cursor movement key to highlight the original expression, as in Figure 5.3. Then press the COPY menu label key (the fourth key in the top row of blank keys) to see the expression redisplayed in the command line (Figure 5.4). To change the angle from 20° to 35°, use the left cursor movement key to highlight the 2 in 20 (Figure 5.5), press the $\boxed{\text{DEL}}$ key twice to delete the two characters, and type in 35. Press the $\boxed{\text{ENTER}}$ key to display the new expression and its approximate value (Figures 5.6 and 5.7).

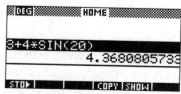

Figure 5.3

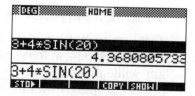

Figure 5.4

Figure 5.5

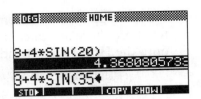

Figure 5.6

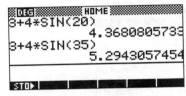

Figure 5.7

As has been mentioned before, all computations are recorded in the Home screen. The computations window will scroll upward to reveal previous calculations that are no longer visible. When you wish to clear all of these calculations from the Home screen, press [CLEAR], which is the blue shift of the [DEL] key. Even after a [CLEAR], the result of the last operation performed is still available to you in the reserved variable *Ans*. The [ANSWER] key, which is the blue shift of the [ENTER] key, allows you access to the contents of this variable. For example, to find the square root of $3 + 4 \sin(35°)$, press the [√x] key, then the blue shift of the [ENTER] key. The calculator pastes in *Ans*, as in Figure 5.8. Press the [ENTER] key to see the result. In addition, the calculator automatically pastes *Ans* into any expression that begins with an operation that requires some antecedent. For example, to now multiply the result by 17, press * 17. The calculator display pastes *Ans*, which in this case is $\sqrt{3 + 4\sin(35)}$, into the command line first, and then follows with the rest (Figure 5.9). Press the [ENTER] key to see the new result, which now, in turn, replaces the old result in the *Ans* register.

Figure 5.8

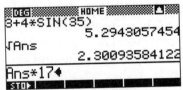

Figure 5.9

Finally, there is one more editing feature of note. Suppose that you are entering an expression with several parentheses, such as $e^{\pi/2^3}$ and you are unsure about where you do and do not need parentheses. Press the blue shift of the [+] key (e^x), and then $(\pi/(2X^y 3))$, even though the parentheses around 2^3 are not necessary (see Figure 5.10). To paste in the symbol π, press the blue shift of the 3 key. When you press the [ENTER] key, the result is displayed, but the editor has cleaned up the expression by removing the superfluous parentheses (Figure 5.11). To see the expression displayed as it would be found in a standard textbook, highlight the expression by pressing the up cursor movement key twice (Figure 5.12) and press the SHOW menu label key. The expression is typeset, as in Figure 5.13. This gives you an easy means of proofreading your expressions for accuracy. Press the OK menu label key to return to the Home screen. Notice that the highlight bar is still on the expression and that there is an arrow in the rightmost quarter of the annunciator bar at the top of the display that is pointing upward. The purpose of this arrow is to remind you that there are more expressions above the computation window that are not presently visible. Depending on where your window is in relation to the entire scrolling screen, you may see a downward pointing window instead, or both.

Press the up cursor movement key three times to see Figure 5.14. Here, we have scrolled to where there are calculations or expressions both above and below the current window onto the Home screen and both arrows are visible in the annunciator bar.

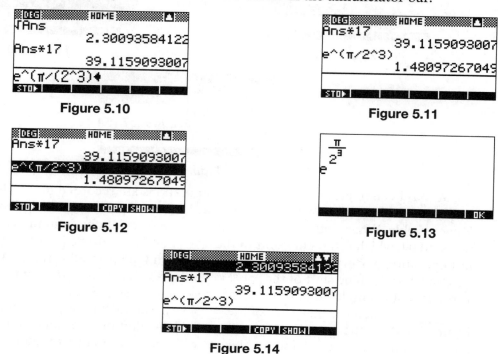

Figure 5.10

Figure 5.11

Figure 5.12

Figure 5.13

Figure 5.14

5.3   Introduction to Aplets

The HP 38G has built-in applications designed to simplify many mathematical processes. These applications are called **Aplets.** Each aplet has graphic, symbolic, and numerical views. The following table lists the title and major uses of each of the native aplets. You may also design and save your own custom aplet.

Aplet Name	Major Purposes
Function	This aplet will plot a graph or build a table based on a function, $y = f(x)$.
Parametric	This aplet plots graphs and builds tables for parametric equations, $x = f_1(t)$ and $y = f_2(t)$.
Polar	This aplet handles polar equations, $r = f(\theta)$.
Sequence	This aplet will plot the staircase graph of a sequence or the cobweb graph of an interactive function. It will also build tables based on a sequence defined by the user.
Solve	This aplet allows you to evaluate expressions and solve equations, including systems of equations.
Statistics	This aplet contains the tools for calculating both one-variable and two-variable statistics. It will also graph scatter plots of data as well as find and plot regression equations.

Whether custom or built-in, aplets may be transferred from one calculator to another via the infrared port located at the top of the calculator. Refer to your owner's manual for information regarding the exchange of aplets. Here, it suffices simply to point out that sending someone an aplet is easy and quick. For example, you might send your Statistics aplet to a colleague, complete with all the data, any regression equation, the plot window settings, and even notes and diagrams. You may even save aplets to a diskette or your computer's hard drive using the connectivity software. In each of the following sections, you will be given a brief tour of one of the built-in aplets.

5.3.1   The Aplet Library Commands

Press LIB, the Aplet Library key, to see the catalog of available aplets (Figure 5.15). Notice the arrow in the bottom right hand corner, indicating that there are more aplets below the viewing window. Also notice the six menu labels. The SAVE command allows you to save any of the built-in aplets in their present state, with whatever equations, window settings, variable values, and notes that are presently set. The RESET command does exactly that, restoring a built-in aplet to its factory settings, clearing out the various equation registers and setting default viewing windows. This command has no effect on custom aplets. The SORT command allows you to sort the aplets, in either alphabetical or chronological order. The SEND and RECV commands control transfer of aplets between calculators or between a calculator and a computer. Finally, the START command allows you to enter an aplet environment.

Figure 5.15

5.3.2   The Solve Aplet

The Solve aplet allows you to work with equations, substituting known values for variables and evaluating the result or solving for a remaining unknown variable. Use the down cursor movement key to highlight the Solve aplet, as in Figure 5.16. Then press the START menu label key to see Figure 5.17. The Solve aplet automatically starts in the Symbolic View which is one of the three views available in each of the aplets. Here, you enter up to ten equations in symbolic form. To return to this view at any time while you are in the Solve aplet, press the SYMB key.

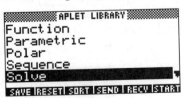

Figure 5.16

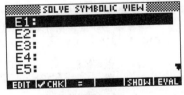

Figure 5.17

Suppose that you wish to find the volume of a cylinder that is 4 meters in height, with a base whose radius is 2 meters. For a right circular cylinder, $V = \pi r^2 h$. Enter this equation in the E1 register using upper case letters for the variables. You will use the shift of the $\boxed{A...Z}$ key to access letters, the third menu label for the equal sign, and the blue shift of the $\boxed{3}$ key for the π character. Your equation should appear in the command line as in Figure 5.18. Notice that the calculator makes the multiplication explicit when you press $\boxed{\text{ENTER}}$, as in Figure 5.19. Also, a check mark is placed to the left of the equation to show that it is the active equation. You may use the CHK menu label key to activate or deactivate any of the ten equations, but only one equation may be active at any given time.

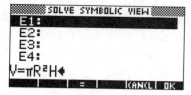

Figure 5.18

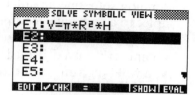

Figure 5.19

Press the [NUM] key to enter the Solve Numeric View (Figure 5.20). In the numeric view, you enter values for known variables and solve for an unknown variable. Use the down cursor movement key to highlight the field for R, the radius, and enter 2, as in Figure 5.21. The highlight bar moves on down to the next variable field in the menu, which is H, the height. Enter 4, as in Figure 5.22. Again, the highlight bar moves on to the next variable in the menu, which is V. This time, since we wish to know the value of V when $r = 2$ and $h = 4$, press the SOLVE menu label key to see the solution, $V = 16\pi \approx 50.265$, as in Figure 5.23.

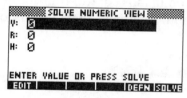

Figure 5.20

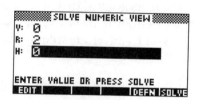

Figure 5.21

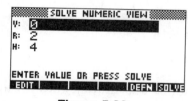

Figure 5.22

Figure 5.23

It is just as easy to solve this equation for r or h as it is to solve it for V. Suppose that you wish to find the radius of a cylinder whose volume is the same as the cylinder above, but whose height is 8 meters. Use the up cursor movement key to highlight the H field and enter 8 (see Figure 5.24). Notice that you do not have to clear out the old value. Just type the replacement value in the command line and press the [ENTER] key or the OK menu label key. Then press the down cursor movement key to bypass the V field, since we want to keep the volume constant. With the highlight bar on the R field, press the SOLVE menu label key. $R = \sqrt{2} \approx 1.414$ appears as the solution as in Figure 5.25.

Figure 5.24

Figure 5.25

To the left of the SOLVE menu label key is the DEFN key, which typesets the symbolic definition of the active equation, in case you are working with several equations and have forgotten which one is currently active. Press the DEFN key now to see our volume formula in Figure 5.26. Press the OK menu label key to return to the numeric view of the Solve aplet.

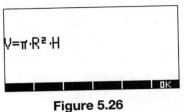

Figure 5.26

We now wish to enter the Plot View of the Solve aplet. Here you may examine the graph of either the radius or height plotted against the volume of the cylinder. With the R field highlighted in the Solve Numeric View menu, press the blue shift of the PLOT key to see the Solve Plot Setup menu. Here we shall set a window for viewing the graph of radius versus volume for cylinders whose heights are all 8 meters.

Set the options in the Solve Plot Setup menu as they appear in Figure 5.27. This is the first of two pages in this menu. Notice the double-width menu label key, PAGE ▼, that allows you to move down to next page in this menu. Press this key to see Figure 5.28. Check marks have been placed to activate certain options. You may change these settings as you see fit using the CHK menu label key.

Figure 5.27

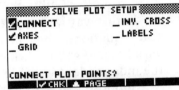

Figure 5.28

Press PLOT to see the graph, as in Figure 5.29. The horizontal line represents the current value of V, about 50.3 m^3. The curve is the plot of radius versus volume, with h held constant at its present value: 8. In other words, the curve is the parabola $V = 8\pi r^2$. In the Solve Plot View, you are automatically tracing. In this case, you are tracing on the line. To move to the curve, press the up or down cursor movement key to move the tracing cursor to the curve (Figure 5.30). Use the left and right cursor movement keys to trace along the curve. Figure 5.31 shows the cursor near our previous solution for V.

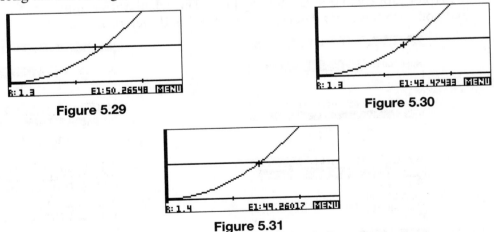

Figure 5.29

Figure 5.30

Figure 5.31

You may also view the plot of height against volume, with the radius held constant at some value. To plot height against volume for cylinders whose radii are all 2 meters, press the NUM key to return to the numeric view. Change the value of R to 2, as in Figure 5.32. Notice that the calculator carried over the last value of r to which we had traced: $r = 1.4$.

With the highlight bar on the H field, return to the Solve Plot Setup menu by pressing the blue shift of the [PLOT] key. We are now plotting height against volume, with the radius held constant at $r = 2$. In other words, we are graphing $V = 4\pi h$. Since this graph is linear, you will need to change the window settings. Figure 5.33 shows one acceptable window. Press [PLOT] to see the graph, as in Figure 5.34. Tracing as before to $H = 4$ shows our first numeric solution of 16π for the volume when $r = 2$ and $h = 4$ (Figure 5.35).

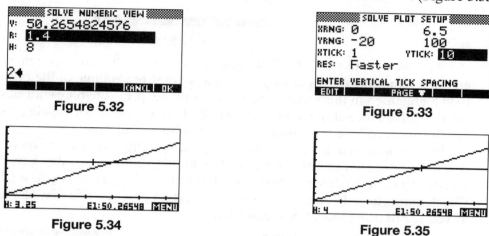

Figure 5.32   Figure 5.33

Figure 5.34   Figure 5.35

In this way, you may examine any two-variable relationship expressed within any of your equations. The calculator will make the left member of the equation the dependent variable and will use whatever variable is highlighted in the Solve Numeric View menu as the independent variable.

Suppose you wish to save these three views with the current equation, window settings, and the values of V, h, and r for later use. Press the LIB key to see the highlight bar still on the Solve aplet. Press the SAVE menu label key to see Figure 5.36. At the prompt, type a new name for this version of the Solve aplet. In this case, we have chosen the name V OF CYLINDER, as in Figure 5.37. Pressing the [ENTER] key pastes the new name into the field and returns you to the Aplet Library, where you can see your new custom aplet (Figure 5.38). Now you may use the Solve aplet for other purposes and still return to the volume formula by starting the V OF CYLINDER aplet. This aplet will remain available to you until you delete it. To delete an aplet, simply highlight its name in the Aplet Library and press the [DEL] key. The calculator prompts you for reassurance that you wish this aplet deleted (Figure 5.39) and then proceeds.

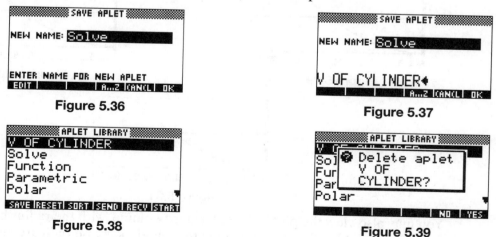

Figure 5.36   Figure 5.37

Figure 5.38   Figure 5.39

Each of the aplets we shall tour in this section has a symbolic view, a numeric view, and a plot view; however, not all the views behave exactly the same as in the Solve aplet.

5.3.3 The Function Aplet

The Function aplet contains tools for graphing and table-building with functions. This section will introduce you to the three views of the Function aplet.

Press the LIB key to enter the Aplet Library, highlight the Function aplet, and press the START menu label key. Like the Solve aplet, the Function aplet starts in the Function Symbolic view, where you can see there are ten function registers (Figure 5.40). Unlike the Solve aplet, as many of these functions as you like may be activated at one time, so that you may plot the graphs of up to ten functions on one screen. Again, the CHK menu label key allows you to activate and deactivate a selection.

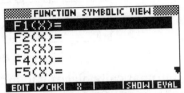

Figure 5.40

Suppose that you wish to plot the graphs of $y = \sin(x)$ and $y = x^2 - 4x + 2$ simultaneously on the same set of axes. With the highlight bar on F1(X), press the ⌈SIN⌉ key and the X menu label key to enter the sine function in register F1. You do not need to enter the closing parenthesis; the HP 38G supplies that for you when you press ⌈ENTER⌉ (or the OK menu label key). After you have entered the first function, the highlight bar moves down to F2(X). Here, enter the quadratic expression $x^2 - 4x + 2$ (Figure 5.41).

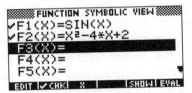

Figure 5.41

When both functions have been entered, press the shift of the SYMB key to enter the Function Symbolic Setup menu. Check here to make sure that angles are being measured in radians. If not, press the CHOOS menu label key and highlight the Radians option, as in Figure 5.42. Press the OK menu label key to accept your selection.

Figure 5.42

Press the shift of the ⌈PLOT⌉ key to enter the Function Plot Setup menu. This menu has two pages, both of which are identical to the corresponding pages in the Solve aplet of the previous section. The first page sets the position of the plotting window and the spacing of ticks along the axes. Pressing the shift of the ⌈DEL⌉ key (CLEAR) will reset all the options to their standard defaults (Figure 5.43). The PAGE ▼ menu label key gives access to the second page of the menu, as in Figure 5.44. Here, the CHK menu label key allows you to choose SIMULT for simultaneous graphing of both functions. By default, it is already active. Press the ⌈PLOT⌉ key to see Figure 5.45.

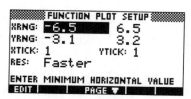

Figure 5.43

Figure 5.44

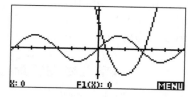

Figure 5.45

The plot window automatically places you in trace mode, with the cursor in the middle of the domain. If more than one function is active, the tracer defaults to the first active function. In this case, $F(X) = \sin(X)$ is the function being traced, as you can see from the labels at the bottom of the screen. Pressing either the up or down cursor movement keys will move the cursor through the cycle of active functions. Press the MENU menu label key to see Figure 5.46. Press the first menu label key, ZOOM, to see the options in the Zoom menu (Figure 5.47). Center will change the plot window's center to the current cursor position and redraw the graphs. Box zooms in on a user-drawn rectangle. In (4 × 4) and Out (4 × 4) zoom in and out by the scaling factors indicated. As you can see in Figure 5.48, you can also zoom in or out along just one or the other of the axes by the indicated scale factor. By default, all of these commands change the center of the plotting window to the current cursor position. To zoom in or out on a particular feature of the graph(s), simply place the cursor on the desired feature and choose the desired zoom option to redraw the graph centered on the desired feature. All subsequent zooms will take this point as their center as long as the cursor has not been moved. Again, this obviously does not apply to the Box zoom option. The last two options are Square and Set Factors (Figure 5.49). Square keeps the current domain, but rescales the range so that the units along both axes are equal in length. Set Factors opens a dialogue box in which you may change the horizontal and vertical zoom factors (Figure 5.50). Notice that this box also contains the RECENTER option. Deactivating this option forces you to manually recenter the plot window on a given feature, using the Center command, before you can zoom in on that feature.

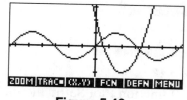

Figure 5.46

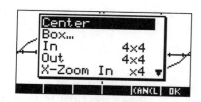

Figure 5.47

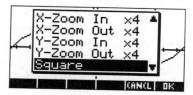

Figure 5.48

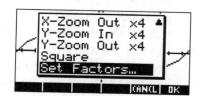

Figure 5.49

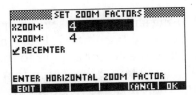

Figure 5.50

Suppose that you wish to zoom in on the second intersection of the curves shown in Figure 5.45 on the previous page. Use the cursor movement keys to move to the Box option of the Zoom menu and press the OK menu label key (Figure 5.51). The calculator prompts you to move the cursor to one of the corners of the zoom box, as in Figure 5.52. Press the OK menu label key and the calculator will prompt you to move the cursor to the diagonally opposite corner of the zoom box. The box is drawn as you move the cursor (Figure 5.53). Pressing the OK menu label key completes the operation. Figure 5.54 shows the plot window after the box zoom. Your graph window may be slightly different.

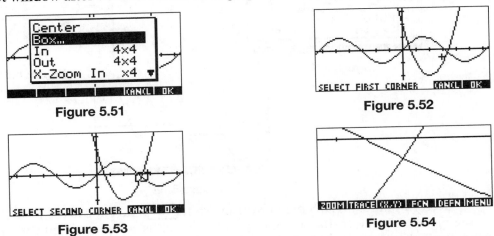

Figure 5.51

Figure 5.52

Figure 5.53

Figure 5.54

There are other options available for controlling the characteristics of the plotting window that are similar to zooms, but are actually preset windows. For example, suppose you wish to establish a window, centered at the origin, that allows each pixel width to represent one unit or one tenth of one unit. These and other so-called friendly windows are contained in the Views menu. But there are more options here than just preset friendly windows. The HP 38G is able to split the screen vertically to show a graph and a zoom or a graph and a table. Before we look at the Views menu and split the screen, we need to reconsider our window settings. In the full screen, there are 130 plotting pixels, so a domain that starts at X = –6.5 and ends at X = 6.5 makes each pixel 0.1 unit wide. In the split screen, there are 64 plotting pixels on either side of a vertical split that is 3 pixels wide. Since the height of the screen remains 63 pixels, the result is a pair of windows that are almost square. With this in mind, return to the Function Plot Setup menu using shift PLOT and change the window settings to agree with Figure 5.55, where each pixel is a 0.1 × 0.1 square.

Figure 5.55

Press VIEWS by using shift ⌐LIB⌐ to see the options shown in Figure 5.56. Now press the OK menu label key to see Figure 5.57. Press the MENU menu label key to restore the menu bar. This time, place the cursor as near to the second point of intersection as possible, press ZOOM, and choose the Zoom In 4 × 4 option. The result is shown in Figure 5.58. Notice the rightmost menu label key: <—. Pressing this key will replace the graph on the left with the zoom on the right, effectively preparing for another zoom. Also note that trace mode is no longer automatically activated. You may activate the tracer by pressing the TRAC menu label key. Activating trace mode does not automatically display the cursor coordinates; to activate cursor coordinate display, whether or not the tracer is enabled, press the (X, Y) menu label key. The cursor moves simultaneously in both halves of the screen. If the tracer is active, then the DEFN menu label key will display the symbolic form of the function being traced.

Figure 5.56

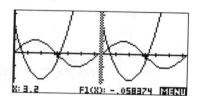

Figure 5.57

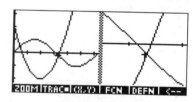

Figure 5.58

Return to the VIEWS menu by using shift ⌐LIB⌐ and choose the Plot-Table option to see Figure 5.59. Here, the previous plot on the left is complemented with a table of values on the right. The tracer has been automatically activated and the table of values reflects the fact that the tracer has chosen the first function in the list of active functions, $F1(X)$. In Figure 5.59, the DEFN menu label key has also been pressed, so that one can see a symbolic as well as a graphic and numeric view of this function. As the tracing cursor is moved on the graph of the function, the highlight bar also moves in the table of values to highlight the current cursor position. In this view, the tracer is always on. As you can see in Figure 5.60, the other options in the Views menu are self-explanatory. **Overlay Plot** allows you to plot one function or set of functions over another. **Auto Scale** keeps the current domain, but chooses a range that will show at least one pixel lit in each pixel column. **Decimal** is the default graphing window, in which each pixel width represents 0.1 units. **Integer** makes each pixel width 1 unit, while **Trig** makes each pixel $\pi/24$ units wide.

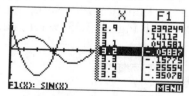

Figure 5.59

Figure 5.60

For example, choose the Trig option and move the cursor to the right 12 times ($12\pi/24 = \pi/2$ units) to see Figure 5.61, in which the cursor sits at $(\pi/2, 1)$ on the $\sin(x)$ function.

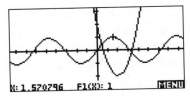

Figure 5.61

With the calculator screen as shown in Figure 5.61, move the cursor a few spaces to the right, press the MENU menu label key, and then press the FCN menu label key to see the Functions menu, as in Figure 5.62. **Root** finds x-intercepts of the function last traced. It does not always find the root nearest the cursor position, especially if the cursor is near a relative maximum or minimum. On the other hand, moving the cursor to one of the pixels adjoining the desired root will suffice for most functions. In this case, since the cursor is somewhere between $\pi/2$ and π, the calculator will find the root at $x = \pi$, as shown in Figure 5.63. To find a root of our quadratic function in $F2(X)$, simply press the down cursor movement key and repeat the steps outlined above.

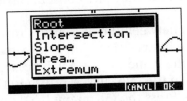

Figure 5.62

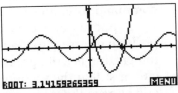

Figure 5.63

Return to the FCN menu by pressing the MENU menu label key and then the FCN menu label key. Move the highlight bar to the **Intersection** command, as in Figure 5.64. This option finds the intersection of the active function and either another function or the x-axis. Press the OK menu label key to see Figure 5.65. Here the message at the top of the choose box indicates that $F1(x) = \sin(x)$ is the active function. The choose box itself prompts you to decide whether you would like the intersection of $F1(x)$ and $F2(x)$ or the x-axis. Choosing the x-axis would amount to the same thing as choosing the **Root** command. Press OK to find the intersection of $F1(x)$ and $F2(x)$ that is closest to the current cursor position at $x = \pi$. The display briefly flashes the message SIGN REVERSAL, as in Figure 5.66, to indicate that the upcoming intersection has been estimated within the limits of the machine's precision. The cursor then moves to the intersection and the estimate is displayed as in Figure 5.67.

Figure 5.64

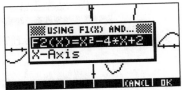

Figure 5.65

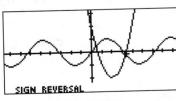

Figure 5.66

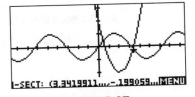

Figure 5.67

Again, return to the FCN menu. There are still three more commands in this menu: **Slope, Area,** and **Extremum.** The slope command calculates the numerical derivative of the active function at the value of x indicated by the current cursor position. Choosing the slope option now (Figure 5.68) will give the slope of the $\sin(x)$ function at the intersection of the two graphs. Since the cursor is close to π and the slope of the $\sin(x)$ function at $x = \pi$ is -1, one would expect a slope value near -1 and such is the case in Figure 5.69.

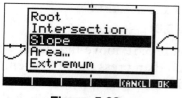

Figure 5.68

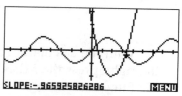

Figure 5.69

Like the Intersection command, the **Area** command starts with the last chosen function and allows the user to choose to estimate the area between that function and the x-axis or between that function and another function. In this way, one may estimate the area under a curve or between two curves. As you will see in the next example, the Area command is sensitive to the order in which the endpoints are chosen. Basically, the Area command estimates the numerical integral.

Suppose that we wish to estimate the area between the two curves from their second positive intersection back to their first positive intersection. Since the direction of integration is from greater to lesser x-values, the value for Area will be negative. With the cursor still at the second positive intersection of the two curves, return to the FCN menu and choose the Area option, as in Figure 5.70. Press the OK menu label key to see Figure 5.71. Since the cursor is already at the desired location, simply press the OK menu label key. The display shows Figure 5.72, where one has the option to choose the area under the $\sin(x)$ function or the area between $F1(x)$ and $F2(x)$. Press OK to choose the area between the curves and move the cursor left until the cursor rests as close as possible to the other chosen intersection (Figure 5.73). Notice that the area is shaded as the cursor moves. Press the OK menu label key to see the area calculated, as in Figure 5.74. Note again that the value for Area is negative, as indicated. Since the cursor coordinates are not displayed, this is only an estimate of the desired area. A more accurate numerical method is available with the integral command (see Section 7.4).

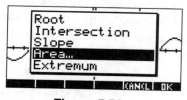

Figure 5.70

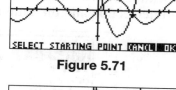

Figure 5.71

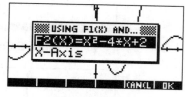

Figure 5.72

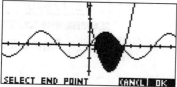

Figure 5.73

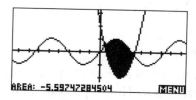

Figure 5.74

Return to the FCN menu one last time and move the highlight bar to the **Extremum** option (Figure 5.75). This command finds both the location and value of the maximum or minimum of the chosen function that is nearest the current cursor location. The cursor is moved to the critical point and the coordinates are displayed at the bottom of the screen, as in Figure 5.76. Since the cursor rests near $x = 0.5$ and the chosen function is still sin(x). the Extremum command in this case found the maximum of sin(x) at $x = \pi/2$. To find the minimum of our quadratic function, simply press the down cursor movement key and repeat the above steps.

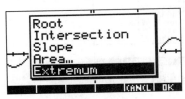

Figure 5.75

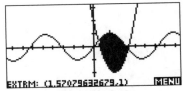

Figure 5.76

Table-building with the HP 38G is as easy as pressing the numerical view key, [NUM]. With the current equations, press the [NUM] key to see Figure 5.77, which shows columns for x, $F1(x)$, and $F2(x)$. You may use the up or down cursor movement keys to move anywhere in a chosen column. Use the left and right cursor movement keys to change columns. If you wish to move quite a ways up or down the column of x-values, there is a nice shortcut. Suppose that you wish to see F1(200) and F2(200). With the cursor anywhere in the x-column, type 200 and press [ENTER]. The table reconfigures itself very quickly, as in Figure 5.78. Notice that the step between the x-values remains 0.1. If you wish to change the step, go to the Function Numeric Setup menu using shift [NUM] to see Figure 5.79. **NUMSTART** controls the first value displayed in the table, although you can always scroll up the table with the up cursor movement key. **NUMSTEP** dictates the change between successive x-values. Set the step to 1 by moving the highlight bar down to highlight the NUMSTEP field, typing 1 and then pressing [ENTER] (Figure 5.80). Press [NUM] now to return to the table and see that the table starts at $x = 200$ and shows only integer values for x (Figure 5.81). Notice that there is a ZOOM menu label key to allow you to zoom in numerically on a chosen value. As you can see from Figure 5.80, the zoom factor is set by default at 4, although you can change it at any time. If you wish to zoom in on the behavior of our function at $x = 202$, for example, move the highlight bar down to that value in the x-column and press the ZOOM menu label key to see Figure 5.82. Here you may choose to zoom IN so that the step between x-values is 0.25 or OUT so that the step is 4. You may also select one of the preset zooms, as in the Views menu. Press the OK menu label key to zoom in so that the x-values step by 0.25, as in Figure 5.83.

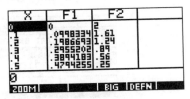

Figure 5.77

Figure 5.78

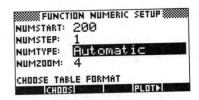

Figure 5.79

Figure 5.80

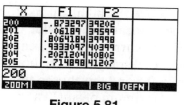

Figure 5.81

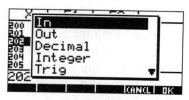

Figure 5.82

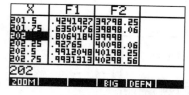

Figure 5.83

Return to the Function Numeric Setup menu and move the highlight bar to the **NUMTYPE** field. Press the CHOOS menu label key to see the options available for the types of tables you can build. There are two types of tables: **Automatic,** the default choice, supplies all the values for all the active functions, as well as the column of x-values. **Build Your Own** leaves the entire table blank to allow you to type in any values for x that you wish. The machine then calculates the function values. Choose this last option and press the NUM key to see Figure 5.84. With the highlight bar anywhere in the x-column, type in any value you please, say 3.85, and press ENTER. The calculator displays F1($-$.650625) and 1.4225 in the $F2$ column, as in Figure 5.85. Notice that the menu label keys have changed once again. The EDIT command allows you to edit any of the x-values. The INS command allows you to insert a new row between any two successive rows. Suppose that you have entered a variety of x-values, as in Figure 5.86. The SORT command will place these x-values in either increasing or decreasing order. In Figure 5.87, the SORT menu label key has been pressed, while in Figure 5.88, the **Ascending** option from the Sort choose box has been chosen. The BIG command increases the display font size and the DEFN command displays the definition of the currently chosen column, much like its counter part in the Plot menu.

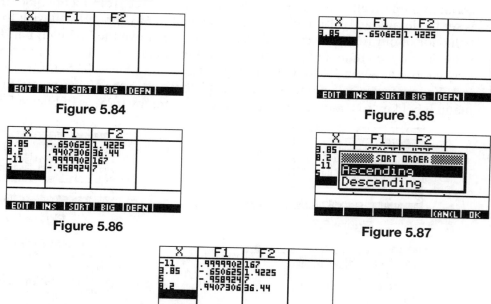

Figure 5.84

Figure 5.85

Figure 5.86

Figure 5.87

Figure 5.88

As with the Solve aplet, you may save the current equations, windows, and other plotting options by pressing the Aplet Library key (LIB), choosing the SAVE option from the menu labels, and typing a new name for your custom function aplet.

5.3.4   The Parametric Aplet

The Parametric aplet does for parametrically defined relations what the Function aplet does for functions defined in Cartesian terms. As in the Function aplet, there are three separate views: symbolic, graphic, and numeric. Another similarity is that both aplets start in the symbolic view, where there are ten equation registers. Go to the Aplet Library menu by pressing the LIB key and move the highlight bar down to the Parametric option. Press the START menu label key to enter the Parametric Symbolic View menu, where you can see the ten empty equation registers.

Suppose that we wish to examine the ellipse defined by the parametric equations $X = 4\cdot\cos(T) - 1$ and $Y = 2\cdot\sin(T) + 1$. With the highlight bar on the $X1(T)$ register, type in the above definition of X and press the [ENTER] key. To insert the variable T, either press the [X,T,θ] key or the T menu label key. The function of the [X,T,θ] key changes with your choice of aplet. In the parametric aplet, it will always insert T. After pressing [ENTER], the highlight bar moves down to the $Y1(T)$ register. Enter our definition of Y and press [ENTER] to see Figure 5.89. Note that the relation is automatically activated after both definitions have been entered, signaled by the check marks placed to the left of the definitions. As in the Function aplet, you may activate or deactivate a relation with the CHK menu label key and as many of the ten possible relations as you wish may be active at one time.

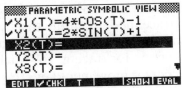

Figure 5.89

Go to the Parametric Symbolic Setup menu using shift [SYMB] and choose the Degrees option for measuring angles in the Angle Measure choose box (Figure 5.90). Then go to the Parametric Plot Setup menu using shift [PLOT] and set the options on the first page to agree with Figure 5.91. Finally, press [PLOT] to see the graph, as in Figure 5.92. As in the Function aplet, Trace mode is automatically enabled and the screen displays both the current value of T as well as the ordered pair that marks the current cursor location. Press the MENU menu label key to see the ZOOM, TRACE, (X, Y), and DEFN menu label keys that operate just as they do in the Function aplet. Notice the absence of the FCN menu, since we are now dealing with relations that may or may not represent functions.

Figure 5.90   **Figure 5.91**

Figure 5.92

Go to the Numeric Setup menu using shift [NUM] and set the NUMSTEP to 1, as in Figure 5.93. Then press the [NUM] key to visit the Numeric View, where you can see the table of T-, X- and Y-values, as shown in Figure 5.94. Again, note that you may zoom in or out on any t-value numerically.

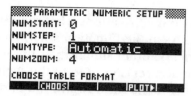

Figure 5.93

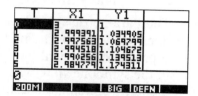

Figure 5.94

5.3.5 The Polar Aplet

The Polar aplet contains the same symbolic, graphic, and numeric views that distinguish the other aplets. This aplet also starts in the symbolic view, where there are ten equation registers.

Go to the Aplet Library menu and move the highlight bar down to the Polar aplet, as in Figure 5.95. Press the START menu label key to see Figure 5.96, which shows the Polar Symbolic View menu. Suppose that we wish to plot the graph of the five-petaled rose $R = 3\sin(5\theta)$ and then circumscribe the circle $R = 3$ around the rose. Enter these equations into the $R1(\theta)$ and $R2(\theta)$ registers, respectively, as shown in Figure 5.97. Go to the Plot Setup menu using shift [PLOT] and set the options on the first page to agree with Figure 5.98. Go to the Views menu using shift [LIB] and choose the Plot-Table option to see Figure 5.99. Here, trace mode is automatically enabled and the highlight bar in the table shows the current cursor position on the active function. By default, $R1(\theta)$ has been chosen as the active function for tracing. To switch both the cursor and the table to $R2(\theta)$, simply press the down cursor movement key. To see the table alone, with both relations showing, enter the Numeric View by pressing the [NUM] key. To see the graph alone, enter the Graphic View by pressing the [PLOT] key.

Figure 5.95

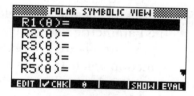

Figure 5.96

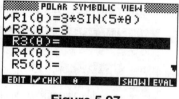

Figure 5.97

Figure 5.98

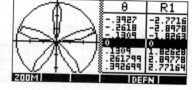

Figure 5.99

As in the other aplets, you may save the present equations and plot settings of this Polar aplet by returning to the Aplet Library menu, pressing the SAVE menu label key, and typing a new name for your custom aplet.

5.4 The Math Commands Menu

In addition to the built-in aplets, the HP 38G makes a wide range of tools available to the mathematician. All of the math functions may be viewed in the Math Functions menu. While there are too many functions available to list and describe them all here, some of the more common ones are shown in Figures 5.100–5.102 below. Press the [MATH] key to see Figure 5.100 below. Move the highlight bar down through the topics listed in the left column to see the commands that are available. Move the highlight bar to the right to highlight a command and then press the OK menu label key to choose a particular function.

Figure 5.100

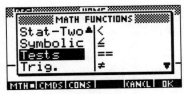

Figure 5.101

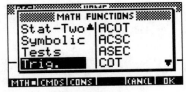

Figure 5.102

For example, suppose we wish to find all roots, real and complex, of the polynomial $x^3 + 2x$. This polynomial has one real root at $x = 0$ and two complex roots, at $x = \pm i\sqrt{2}$. Figure 5.103 shows the **POLYROOT** command being selected, while Figure 5.104 shows the coefficients of the polynomial entered in a matrix as the argument for this command. Finally, Figure 5.105 shows the first and second solutions, with the ellipsis indicating that there is another solution that is not being displayed.

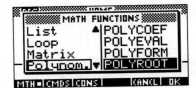

Figure 5.103

Figure 5.104

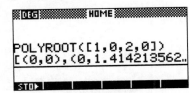

Figure 5.105

5.5   Conclusion

The reader is urged to browse through the owner's manual to see all of the commands available. The reader is also encouraged to explore the other aplets, especially the Sequence and Statistics aplets.

Answers
Grapher Workshop

■ Section 1.1 Exercises for Chapter 1
(pp. 20–24)

The graphs used in these answers are from the Texas
Instruments TI-83 graphing calculator and are similar to
the ones that would appear on the Sharp and most Casio
graphing calculators. Use Table 1.4 to convert special
viewing windows (decimal, friendly, etc.) to appropriate
ones for your graphing calculator if it is not one of these.

1. 693.375

2. 3.71293

3. −1

4. 7

5. 4

6. 3

7. 2, 12, 72, 432, 2592, 15552, 93312

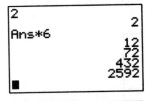

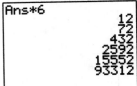

8. 4, 13, 22, 31, 40, 49, 58

9. 4, 1.75, 10

```
-3→X:X²+X-2
              4
-2.5→X:X²+X-2
            1.75
3→X:X²+X-2
             10
■
```

10. −26, 61.608, 651

```
-2→T:2T³-abs(5T
             -26
3.4→T:2T³-abs(5T
          61.608
7→T:2T³-abs(5T
             651
```

11. a.
```
  X   | Y1
 -3   | 24
 -2   | 19
 -1   | 16
  0   | 15
  1   | 16
  2   | 19
  3   | 24
Y1■X²+15
```

b.
```
  X   | Y1
  0   | 15
  1   | 16
  2   | 19
  3   | 24
  4   | 31
  5   | 40
  6   | 51
Y1■X²+15
```

c.
```
  X   | Y1
-10   | 115
 -5   | 40
  0   | 15
  5   | 40
 10   | 115
 15   | 240
 20   | 415
Y1■X²+15
```

12. a.
```
  X   | Y1
 -3   | 2.3026
 -2   | 1.6094
 -1   | .69315
  0   | 0
  1   | .69315
  2   | 1.6094
  3   | 2.3026
Y1■ln(X²+1)
```

b.
```
  X   | Y1
  0   | 0
  1   | .69315
  2   | 1.6094
  3   | 2.3026
  4   | 2.8332
  5   | 3.2581
  6   | 3.6109
Y1■ln(X²+1)
```

c.
```
  X   | Y1
-10   | 4.6151
 -5   | 3.2581
  0   | 0
  5   | 3.2581
 10   | 4.6151
 15   | 5.4205
 20   | 5.994
Y1■ln(X²+1)
```

13. a.
```
  X   | Y1
 -3   | 5
 -2   | 4
 -1   | 3
  0   | 2
  1   | 1
  2   | 0
  3   | 1
Y1■abs(X-2)
```

b.

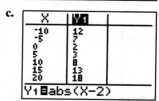

c.

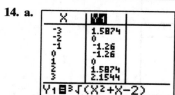

14. a.

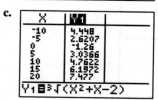

b.

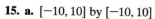

c.

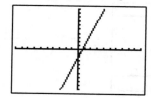

15. a. [−10, 10] by [−10, 10]

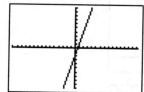

b. [−15.161..., 15.161...] by [−10, 10]

c & d. [−4.7, 4.7] by [−3.1, 3.1] On the TI-83, Casio, and Sharp graphing calculators, the decimal window is square and friendly. This is not true on all graphers. For example, the decimal window on the TI-85 is friendly but not square.

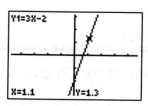

16. a. [−10, 10] by [−10, 10]

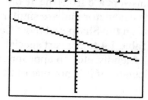

b. [−15.161..., 15.161...] by [−10, 10]

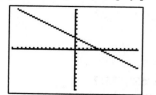

c. [−9.4, 9.4] by [−5, 10]

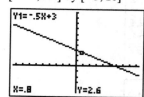

d. [−9.4, 9.4] by [−6.2, 6.2]

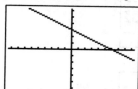

17. a. [−10, 10] by [−10, 10]

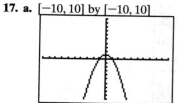

b. [−15.161..., 15.161...] by [−10, 10]

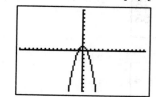

c. & d. [−4.7, 4.7] by [−3.1, 3.1]

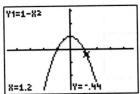

18. a. [−10, 10] by [−10, 10]

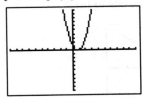

b. [−15.161..., 15.161...] by [−10, 10]

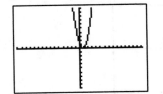

c. & d. [−4.7, 4.7] by [−3.1, 3.1]

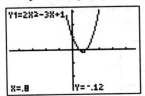

19. a. [−10, 10] by [−10, 10]

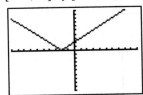

b. [−15.161..., 15.161...] by [−10, 10]

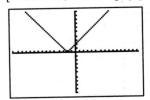

c. & d. [−4.7, 4.7] by [−3.1, 3.1]

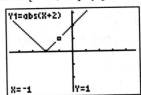

20. a. [−10, 10] by [−10, 10]

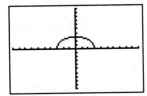

b. [−15.161..., 15.161...] by [−10, 10]

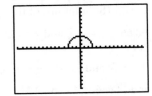

c. & d. [−4.7, 4.7] by [−3.1, 3.1]

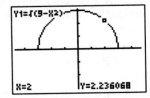

21. In sequential mode, first the graph of y_1 is drawn, then the graph of y_2, and finally the graph of y_3. In simultaneous mode, the three graphs are drawn at the same time.

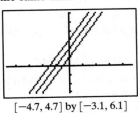

[−4.7, 4.7] by [−3.1, 6.1]

22. In dot mode, one point is plotted in each column of pixels provided the point is in the viewing window. That is, if the corresponding y-value lies between Ymin and Ymax. In connected mode, points are plotted and joined together to produce a line that appears to have no breaks in it.

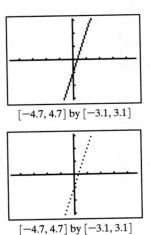

[−4.7, 4.7] by [−3.1, 3.1]

[−4.7, 4.7] by [−3.1, 3.1]

23. One possibility is $[-10, 15]$ by $[-300, 200]$. There are two x-intercepts.

24. One possibility is $[-15, 5]$ by $[-2200, 500]$. There are three x-intercepts.

25. a. The graphs of $y_1 = |x|$ and $y_2 = \frac{1}{2}x + 1$

   intersect at $(-0.666\ldots, 0.666\ldots)$ and $(2, 2)$.

   b. The x-intercepts of $y_3 = y_1 - y_2$ are $x = -0.666\ldots$ and $x = 2$. The solutions of the equations are $x = -0.666\ldots = -\frac{2}{3}$ and $x = 2$.

26. a. The graphs of $y_1 = |x - 3|$ and $y_2 = -\frac{1}{2}x + 4$

   intersect at $(-2, 5)$ and $(4.666\ldots, 1.666\ldots)$.

   b. The x-intercepts of $y_3 = y_1 - y_2$ are $x = -2$ and $x = 4.666\ldots$. The solutions of the equation are $x = -2$ and $x = 4.666\ldots = 4\frac{2}{3}$.

27. a. The graphs of $y_1 = x - 2$ and $y_2 = 1 - x^2$ intersect at $(-2.303\ldots, -4.303\ldots)$ and $(1.303\ldots, -0.697\ldots)$.

   b. The x-intercepts of $y_3 = y_1 - y_2$ are $x = -2.303\ldots$ and $x = 1.303\ldots$. The solutions of the equation are $x \approx -2.303$ and $x \approx 1.303$.

28. a. The graphs of $y_1 = x - 3$ and $y_2 = x^2 - 5$ intersect at $(-1, -4)$ and $(2, -1)$.

   b. The x-intercepts of $y_3 = y_1 - y_2$ are $x = -1$ and $x = 2$. The solutions of the equation are $x = -1$ and $x = 2$.

29. a. One possibility is $[-10, 15]$ by $[-300, 200]$.

   b. There is a local maximum of 0 at $x = 0$, and a local minimum of -256 at $x = 8$.

30. a. One possibility is $[-15, 5]$ by $[-2200, 500]$.

   b. Accurate to two decimal places there is a local minimum of -2112.40 at $x = -11.05$, a local maximum of 0 at $x = -3$, and a local minimum of -52.10 at $x = -0.95$. (You may need to zoom-in to find these values.)

31. All graphs are drawn in the $[-12, 12]$ by $[-12, 12]$ viewing window.

a.

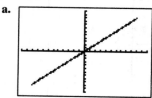

b.

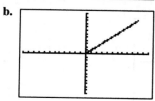

c.

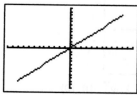

d. This graph may appear to be the same as in (a), but there are fewer points plotted. Also this graph is drawn faster than the one in (a).

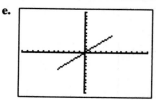

e.

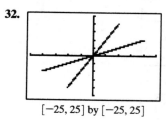

f. Same as (a), except this graph is drawn from upper right to lower left, and the graph in (a) is drawn from lower left to upper right.

32.

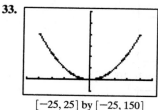

$[-25, 25]$ by $[-25, 25]$

33.

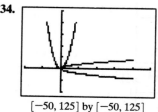

$[-25, 25]$ by $[-25, 150]$

34.

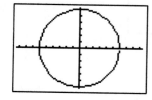

$[-50, 125]$ by $[-50, 125]$

35. Viewing window: $[-9.4, 9.4]$ by $[-6.2, 6.2]$, $\theta\text{min} = 0$, $\theta\text{max} = 2\pi$, $\theta\text{step} = 0.1$.

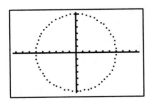

36. Viewing window: [–4.7, 4.7] by [–3.1, 3.1], θmin = 0, θmax = π, θstep = 0.1.

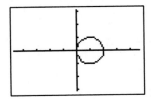

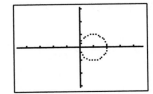

37. Viewing window: [–9.4, 9.4] by [–6.2, 6.2], θmin = 0, θmax = 2π, θstep = 0.1.

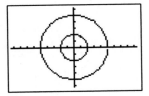

38. Viewing window: [–4.7, 4.7] by [–3.1, 3.1], θmin = 0, θmax = 2π, θstep = 0.1.

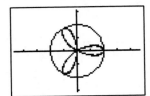

39. b.

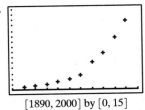

[1890, 2000] by [0, 15]

c.

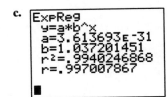

```
ExpReg
 y=a*b^x
 a=3.613693E-31
 b=1.037201451
 r²=.9940246868
 r=.997007867
■
```

d.

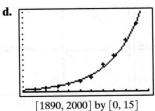

[1890, 2000] by [0, 15]

40. b.

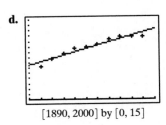

[1890, 2000] by [0, 15]

c.

```
LinReg
 y=ax+b
 a=.0612121212
 b=-109.0975758
 r²=.9304153989
 r=.9645804263
```

d.

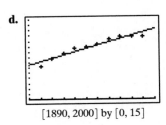

[1890, 2000] by [0, 15]

41. a. det A = 17

  b. $A^{-1} = \begin{pmatrix} 2/17 & 3/17 \\ -5/17 & 1/17 \end{pmatrix}$

  c. $A^{-1}B = \begin{pmatrix} 2 \\ 1 \end{pmatrix}$

42. a. det A = −33

  b. $A^{-1} = \begin{pmatrix} 5/33 & 13/33 & 1/33 \\ 5/33 & -20/33 & 1/33 \\ -1/11 & 4/11 & 2/11 \end{pmatrix}$

  c. $A^{-1}B = \begin{pmatrix} 3 \\ 1 \\ -1 \end{pmatrix}$

43.

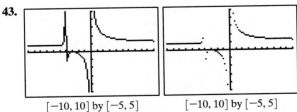

[−10, 10] by [−5, 5]   [−10, 10] by [−5, 5]

44.

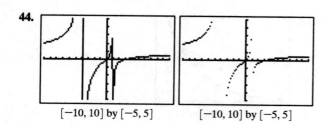

[−10, 10] by [−5, 5]   [−10, 10] by [−5, 5]